THE

QUOTABLE

GIULIANI

★

THE
QUOTABLE
GIULIANI

---- ★ ----

*The Mayor of America
in His Own Words*

EDITED BY
BILL ADLER
AND
BILL ADLER, JR.

POCKET BOOKS
New York   London   Toronto   Sydney   Singapore

An *Original* Publication of POCKET BOOKS

 POCKET BOOKS, a division of Simon & Schuster, Inc.
1230 Avenue of the Americas, New York, NY 10020

ISBN: 0-7434-5417-0

First Pocket Books trade paperback printing April 2002

10 9 8 7 6 5 4 3 2 1

POCKET and colophon are a registered trademarks of
Simon & Schuster, Inc.

For information regarding special discounts for bulk purchases,
please contact Simon & Schuster Special Sales at 1-800-456-6798
or business@simonandschuster.com

Front cover photo: AP/Wide World Photos/Kathy Willens
Back cover photo: AP/Wide World Photos/Doug Mills
Interior design by Jaime Putorti

Printed in the U.S.A.

Contents

★ Contents ★

Introduction

A lifelong New Yorker, Rudolph "Rudy" Giuliani was born, raised, and educated in New York, which he served for two terms as mayor, 1994–2001. Fiercely committed to New York since growing up a New York Yankee fan in the shadow of the Brooklyn Dodgers' Ebbets Field, Giuliani attended Bishop Loughlin Memorial High School in Brooklyn on an academic scholarship, graduating in 1961 with the title of "Class Politician." He moved on to Manhattan College, and, after briefly considering the priesthood, decided on a career in law. He was selected to the prestigious *Law Review* during his first year at New York University Law School, from which he graduated magna cum laude in 1968.

After serving as assistant U.S. attorney for the Southern District of New York, executive assistant U.S. attorney, and then associate deputy attorney general, Giuliani was appointed associate attorney general in 1981, the number three position in President Ronald Reagan's administration.

Returning to New York in 1983 to an appointment as U.S. attorney for the Southern District of New York, Giuliani forged a reputation as a "no regrets" prosecutor, earning note-worthy prosecutions against Wall Street's inside traders, the Mafia, and corrupt government officials.

Never one to give up a battle, Giuliani was elected 107th mayor of the city of New York on November 2, 1993, after first being defeated by David Dinkins by less than fifty thousand votes four years earlier in 1989.

Giuliani delivered on his campaign promises to clean up the streets of New York and to improve the quality of life, ridding the city of intimidating squeegee men who had become a city fixture, graffiti vandals, drug dealers, and perpetrators of the highest levels of crime. During his two terms, crime dropped by about 64 percent. He called the idea that New York City was unmanageable, ungovernable "politically incorrect."

Accusations of police misconduct and an unsuccessful battle to abolish the city's Board of Education plagued his term, but his record of remarkable crime reduction and improvements to quality of life earned him reelection on November 4, 1997, in a landslide victory over Democratic challenger Ruth Messinger. Not since Fiorello LaGuardia's reelection in 1941 had New York City elected a Republican mayor to a second term.

New York City was again livable, crime had been reduced dramatically, jobs were being created, more and more people were moving off welfare, and even Times Square had become family-friendly after a ban on sex shops. The mayor was eyeing a New York Senate race in 2000, in which he was to challenge First Lady Hillary Rodham Clinton, the first wife of a sitting president to run for public office. Calling the potential race "terrific," Giuliani withdrew his bid on May 19, 2000, after announcing that he had been diagnosed with a treatable form of prostate cancer. "It brings up very painful memories," he said, recounting his father's death from the disease in 1981. He vowed to make the most of his remaining eighteen months in office and to put his health before further political pursuits.

His battle against cancer, however, would not be his last while in office. On the morning of September 11, 2001, just three months shy of the end of his term, the life of the mayor, the life of the city he proudly called the "capital of the world," and the life of the nation would forever be changed after simultaneous terrorist attacks on the Pentagon in Washington, D.C., and the twin towers of the World Trade Center, which both collapsed after two hijacked aircraft crashed into them.

Giuliani narrowly escaped death himself after being trapped briefly in a nearby building as the first tower collapsed. In the worst terrorist attack ever on American soil, New York City was devastated by the loss of almost 3,000 innocent victims of terror—including 343 firefighters, 23 police officers—and the change in its skyline.

For his immediate resilience and determination, for his strong leadership of a stunned city and country, for his compassion to a city in mourning, he was recognized as a great leader in the face of crisis and affectionately labeled "America's Mayor." His father's advice "to remain calm and to actually become calmer as things around you are getting more and more out of control" was never more needed and heeded. Giuliani urged the city to get back to business and to rise above terror, even when that seemed impossible amid such incomprehensible devastation. Determined to rid the world of terror, the tough prosecutor also showed that it was okay to cry, to grieve, to react.

Though barred by term limits to run again for mayor, Giuliani considered seeking legislation to extend his term or to run for a third term on the Conservative Party ticket. Deciding instead that he did not want to divide the city, he endorsed Michael Bloomberg, elected the 108th mayor of the city of New York and sworn in by Giuliani in an historic Times Square ceremony as 2002 and the rebuilding of New York officially began under Bloomberg.

Chants of "Rudy! Rudy! Rudy!" greeted Giuliani as he left office with a high approval rating. The city of New York recognized not just a great leader in time of crisis but also a mayor who had worked so hard for the city and the people he so loved throughout his eight years in office.

"I think the first thing he did is make New York believe in itself again," observed close friend and former deputy mayor Peter Powers.

And now, the "Mayor of America" remembers his life, his career, his time as mayor to the city and the country, in his own words.

PART I

GIULIANI ON SEPTEMBER 11

★

1

The Morning of
September 11

———— ★ ————

Giuliani was having breakfast at the Peninsula Hotel on Fifth Avenue in midtown Manhattan on the morning of September 11 when his aide Dennison Young, Jr., received the phone call that the World Trade Center had been attacked. Giuliani remembers:

★ My first thought is sort of a rejection: How could this happen? Airplanes don't hit the World Trade Center. What are we talking about?

★ How could anyone do this to my city?

*Shortly after arriving at the disaster site, the mayor
recounts the tragedy he witnessed.*

★ I get the first real view of the building and see that, no matter
how it was described, it's much worse. The top of the building is
totally in flames. I look up, and for some reason my eye catches the
top of the World Trade Center, and I see a man jump—it must
have been at least one hundred stories up.... When I look around,
what I see is something close to a nuclear bomb. I see dark smoke.

On arriving at the World Trade Center collapse:

★ Just pray to God that we can save a few people.

Recounting his route to safety:

★ We were on a ground floor that had windows and you could
look outside. All of a sudden, it became black, and then white.
And things were pelting down. I heard things hitting the building. We went down to the basement to exit. We tried one exit. It
was locked. We tried another exit. That was locked. And then [a
security guard] decided to come back upstairs. He said, "There's
an exit upstairs. We can go out through the upstairs area." When
we came upstairs, back into the area we had been in originally,
things had gotten worse. There was smoke outside; it was much
heavier. There was much more debris falling. And the exit on the
main floor was closed. A security guard then came up to us and
said, "I think we can go out through the adjoining building. I
think that's open." So we all went back downstairs, tried another
exit. That didn't work. And then, finally, he went to an exit and
he opened it. And we walked through into the lobby of 100 Park
Place, which is an adjoining building that faces east. When that
door opened, I think all of us breathed a sigh of relief, although
when we got into the lobby, I wasn't sure we were better off,
because when we looked outside, it looked like Armageddon. It
was black and white, and there was no visibility at all.

To Police Commissioner Bernard Kerik on the morning of September 11:

★ How the hell did they get the Pentagon?

At the base of the World Trade Center moments before the towers collapsed, Giuliani encountered New York City Fire Department Chaplain and close friend Father Mychal Judge, one of the first killed in the collapse while administering last rites to a firefighter.

★ "Pray for us," asked Giuliani.
   "I always do," assured Judge.

Soon after, Judge was killed by debris after removing his hat to pray. Giuliani later said of Judge, "He was a saint, a wonderful man."

September 11, 10:54 A.M.:

★ I've never seen anything like this. I was there from shortly after it happened and saw people jumping out of the World Trade Center. It's a horrible, horrible situation, and . . . every resource that we have is attempting to rescue as many people as possible. And the end result is going to be some horrendous number of lives lost. I don't think we know yet, but right now we have to just focus on saving as many people as possible.

★ It was the most horrific scene I've ever seen in my whole life. We saw the World Trade Center in flames, a big, gaping hole all the way to the top of it.

★ I think what horrifies me the most is that moments after the attack you saw people jumping out of the window. It's an image that I keep getting . . . that I saw a man jumping out of the top of the World Trade Center, just hurl himself out the window and come down a . . . hundred floors. When I saw that . . . I said to myself, "We are in something now that is totally different than anything that we've ever imagined before."

On being asked by ABC News's Barbara Walters in the days after the attacks to recount his most "searing" memories of September 11:

★ I don't even know what comes first. Seeing a man jumping from the top of the World Trade Center, being trapped for a while . . . in the basement, being told that the World Trade Center was collapsing, which was something you couldn't possibly believe would happen. Hearing an airplane overhead, and first having someone yell out, "There's another airplane attacking," and then have someone else say, "It's one of ours." Going to the morgue now and seeing what they're going through, or to the site where people there are just hoping and hoping and hoping that they're going to find some . . . people that are alive, with the hope of that diminishing.

On being asked by Barbara Walters if he thought he was going to die on the morning of September 11:

★ Now I do, when I think back on it. That night and the next day, now when I think back on it, I realize that we were in a lot of danger. But at the time, there really wasn't time to think about it. And I don't think until we walked out into the Park Place building—I don't think I realized how bad it was . . . We were right behind 7 World Trade Center. And 7 World Trade Center absorbed the biggest hit from the fallen building, and probably saved our life.

On being asked in a September 11 press conference what went through his mind as he was trying to escape to safety earlier that morning:

★ I don't think anything went through my mind, other than making sure that we all remained calm and found an exit and just tried to figure out the most intelligent thing to do, probably the same thing that went through the minds of ten thousand other New Yorkers who I could see on the streets.

Giuliani became the voice of the nation as the Secret Service rushed to assure President Bush's safety at a secure location. Giuliani was both fierce at the terror attack and comforting to a nation in mourning. In a September 11 press conference, Giuliani addressed the nation and became the "Mayor of America."

★ And we will strive now very hard to save as many people as possible, and to send a message that the city of New York and the United States of America is much stronger than any group of barbaric terrorists; that our democracy, that our rule of law, that our strength and our willingness to defend ourselves will ultimately prevail.

★ This has been a very, very difficult and traumatic day for the people of the United States and the people of the city.

★ This is a tragedy that we thought would never happen.

★ People tonight should say a prayer for the people that we've lost and be grateful that we're all here. And tomorrow, New York is going to be here. And we're going to rebuild and we're going to be stronger than we were before.

★ The city is going to survive. We're going to get through it. It's going to be a very difficult time. I don't think we yet know the pain we're going to feel when we find out who we lost. But the thing we have to focus on now is getting the city through this and surviving and being stronger for it.

★ Nobody should blame any group of people or any nationality or any ethnic group.

★ If you really want to know what New Yorkers are all about, you just watch the way in which they handled themselves. They didn't panic. They moved deliberately. They moved swiftly. But they didn't hurt each other; they helped each other. I mean, these are just the most wonderful people in the world.

★ This is a vicious, unprovoked, horrible attack on innocent men, women, and children. It's one of the most heinous acts certainly in world history.

★ I believe that the people in New York City can demonstrate our resolve and our support for all of the people that were viciously attacked today by going about their lives and showing everyone that vicious, cowardly terrorists can't stop us from being a free country and a place that functions. And we'll do everything we can to make that point.

★ Everybody should in their own way say a prayer and ask God for help and for assistance, and also ask God to give us the strength to overcome this, because I know we're going to need strength to overcome it.

★ And I want the people of New York to be an example to the rest of the country and the rest of the world, that terrorism can't stop us. American democracy is much stronger than vicious, cowardly terrorists, and we're going to overcome this.

★ And as the governor said and I said to the president, we fully and completely support him in any action that he has to take in order to make an example out of the people who are responsible for this.

2

"America's Mayor"— Leading a City and a Nation Through Crisis

———————— ★ ————————

Just three months before the end of his term, Giuliani was lauded for the strength and courage he displayed and encouraged in others in the days, weeks, and months following the attacks.

From a September 12, 2001, press conference:

★ The best way they can deal with this right now is not only to deal with their own grief, which we all feel and have, but to show that we're not going to be in any way affected by this. That we're not going to be cowarded by it. That we're not afraid. That we're going to go about our business and lead normal lives and not let these cowards affect us in any way like they're trying to do, which is to instill fear in us.

*On being asked during the briefing about the search efforts
for survivors of the World Trade Center collapse the day
after the attacks:*

★ We still have not given up hope.

Forty-eight hours after the attacks:

★ The terrible reality of this is we may never be able to
recover everyone. We're going to try.

*At a press conference announcing the reopening of the New
York Stock Exchange following September 11:*

★ We understand even more the value of our democracy. We
appreciate even more a nation that's ruled by law and decency
and concern for human life, and we understand what's necessary to defend ourselves, our values, and our children. And the
American people are united as never before.

*On the September 13, 2001, reopening of the New York
Stock Exchange:*

★ It's going to be difficult, but I believe we can do it, and I
believe it would be a good thing to do, a really good thing to
do.

En route to the New York Stock Exchange opening following the attacks, the mayor spoke of the building where President George Washington was inaugurated.

★ This was the first capital of the United States. All of those . . . buildings were in the Wall Street area. So in addition to being the financial capital of the United States and the world, Wall Street is a monument to our liberty.

At a September 15 news conference:

★ And I think people should be mournful and sorrowful, but they should also be very encouraged that we have tremendous courage in New York, we have tremendous courage in America, and the courage will be there in our generation as it was in prior generations.

★ We're going to try to save human life until we're told that that's impossible.

At a September 18 news conference, preparing people for the grim loss:

★ We have to prepare people for the overwhelming reality that the chance of recovering anyone alive is very, very small. We still hope and pray.

★ I was so proud of the people I saw on the street. No chaos, but they were frightened and confused, and it seemed to me that they needed to hear from my heart where I thought we were going. I was trying to think, "Where can I go for some comparison to this, some lessons about how to handle it?" So I started thinking about Churchill, started thinking that we're going to have to rebuild the spirit of the city, and what better example than Churchill and the people of London during the Blitz in 1940 who had to keep up their spirit during this sustained bombing? It was a comforting thought.

When told that it would take ten days to clean up one of the buildings at the World Trade Center wreckage, Giuliani rallied his troops.

★ It took God seven days to create the earth. So we can do better than that, don't you think?

On leading New York City out of tragedy:

★ You just get up and do it. You find that you don't want to sleep; you want to get up and do things that have to be done.

★ I can't think of a city or of a place that could have been attacked the way New York City was and responded as quickly, with as much resoluteness and determination and patriotism as the people of New York City. And I've always been proud of them and loved them, and I think I'm even prouder of them than I've ever been before. And they've more than exceeded my expectations of how they would have reacted to something like this.

★ Whatever strength I have is from the people of New York.

★ We're going to take care of this. We'll make things right.

On combining leadership in the September 11 recovery effort:

★ We all have different resources and different things that we can bring to this. If we all work together, the city is going to get through this, the people of the city are going to get through it, and the city of New York is going to demonstrate that a free democratic society can absorb this kind of blow and become stronger by it, and we're going to foil the desires of these cowards who attacked us.

Addressing President George W. Bush in the days following the World Trade Center collapse:

★ The work you've done for us we all eternally appreciate. You've been a terrific leader and we're taking direction from you and we're following your example. You've done a terrific job, Mr. President.

On Washington, D.C.'s assistance following the attacks:

★ There hasn't been a single thing that we have needed and asked for that we haven't gotten, and more.

Putting politics aside, Giuliani praised President George W. Bush during his November 11 tribute to the victims of September 11.

★ Mr. President, this city is united. As Americans, we're also united behind you as our leader. I want you to know that this city that didn't vote for you is in love with you and you're doing an absolutely great job.

On learning Queen Elizabeth II had selected him for honorary knighthood:

★ I feel it is for everyone. I am sure I speak for the police commissioner and the fire commissioner when I say that this award, and these awards, are really for the actions of the people of our city. We are very gratified by this but we see it as an award being given to all the people of New York City.

★ Please convey to the queen that I'm humbled and that we feel the awards are really for the reaction of all the people of New York City who handled the worst attack on America with great bravery and dignity and helped to inspire an entire country.

On being asked if he wanted to be called "Sir Rudolph":

★ Just call me Rudy.

Giuliani then went on to praise the efforts of England following the September 11 attacks.

★ From the moment this happened, we could not have had a more loyal friend or a stronger support than the British government. It has been a great support for us.

In October 2001, on receiving the Cavaliere di Gran Croce, Italy's highest civilian honor, from deputy prime minister of Italy, Gianfranco Fini, for his leadership following the September 11 attacks:

★ I'm very humbled.

On his leadership style in the wake of tragedy:

★ You have to try to be what you have to be in order to be a leader. . . . There are times in which you have to be combative, and there are times in which you have to be controversial if you believe in something. And then there are times in which you have to try to unify. And there's no choice now. . . . I can be pretty combative if you point me in the right direction, right now. But when they attack us, we're all together. And right now, we're all together.

On defending his reduction in the number of World Trade Center recovery workers after protests by firefighters:

★ There is something that I have to worry about that, no matter all the screaming, yelling, distortion, or lying that is going on . . . and that is the safety of the people undertaking this mission.

*On being asked by Barbara Walters if the time following
September 11 was his finest hour:*

★ It's my most difficult time . . . I have no doubt that it's the
finest hour for the city of New York . . . I have no question
about that. I think that it's its worst hour and its finest hour.
And I have no doubt that the city's going to build on that
strength that it's acquired from this and be even a much
greater city in the future than it's been in the past.

From his November 2001 weekly column:

★ As mayor, I have never been more proud to represent this
great city, and I am confident that our perseverance and determination will bring us even more success in the years to come.

★ They really don't know how badly they were attacked. Two
of our largest buildings get destroyed, thousands of people
dead, more than that injured. And here they are, back on track
with their lives—enthusiastic, exceedingly patriotic, more
united, defiant. And I just reflected that. People ask me how I
do it: I just reflect the way they are.

★ I don't believe that I've changed. On September 11, 12, 13,
I did the same things . . . the same things I've done when we've
had fires and catastrophes . . . except it was on a different scale.

★ I'd feel very bad if I were described as a hero. I'm just
a reflection of the real heroes who have risked their lives for
others.

3

The Heroes of September 11

────────── ★ ──────────

In praise of the New York City Fire Department, New York City Police Department, Port Authority police, EMS workers, court officers, and other emergency personnel who helped in September 11 rescue efforts:

★ We will never know all the details of the heroism that occurred on September 11. But we know that because of the actions of our fire department, police department, Port Authority Police Department, EMTs and court officers, twenty-five thousand more people are alive today. In tribute to the memory of these patriots, we should always remember that ground zero does not just mark the site of tragedy, but the greatest and most successful rescue operation in American history.

★ Not a single one of those heroes died in vain. Their courage, selflessness, and professionalism saved more than twenty-five thousand lives that day. . . . These were true American patriots. They gave their lives in defense of liberty.

★ They're the people who deserve all the credit, all the praise, and all the support.

★ They saved us on Tuesday. They brought us back on Wednesday. And they're protecting us today.

★ The rescue efforts are nothing short of miraculous.

★ The men and women who are doing this rescue effort are very dedicated and they're terrific. . . . They are literally putting their lives at risk to try to find people and save them. . . . So, when you see them operating and working, realize how dedicated they are.

When asked about the determination of the firefighters and World Trade Center rescuers during an October 2001 Larry King Live *appearance:*

★ . . . They're amazing. Absolutely amazing.

★ What happened here is enormously personal. There are . . . different emotions that emerge. Sorrow and mourning, anger, tremendous anger, and then pride, tremendous pride at what those firefighters accomplished. . . . They did not die in vain. They saved over twenty-five thousand people, and they defended freedom and gave us an example of how far we're going to have to defend ourselves and fight back and end terrorism. No ifs, ands, or buts about it. We have to end it.

★ The greatest single rescue mission in America's history: They knew what they were up against, but they went in anyway. That's what heroes do.

★ Inspired by their examples of bravery, we need to move forward—in defiance of terror—to show the world that a free, inclusive, and civil society will triumph over all forms of tyranny.

★ We've had fire departments from Chicago, Philadelphia, Los Angeles, Sacramento, and so many other places help us . . . it really is quite impressive, and it's a wonderful outpouring of care and concern for the city of New York.

★ The magnitude of the horror is still hard to comprehend. Those proud twin towers that crowned our skyline for a quarter century no longer stand. Even more devastating is the loss of thousands of individuals who were killed in the attacks. All were innocent. All were heroes.

★ These people didn't die so that we would let terrorists control our lives. That isn't the reason they died. Terry Hatton and Ray Downey and Pete Ganci . . . didn't die so that . . . we wouldn't go on airplanes anymore or we'd be afraid to walk around the streets or afraid to go to restaurants. They died so that America would be free, America would have the ability to function . . . that's what they want.

★ Those who went to work in the World Trade Center on September 11 were engaged in the quiet heroism of supporting their families, pursuing their dreams, and playing their own meaningful part in a diverse, dynamic, and free society. We will never know many of the selfless acts of courage that occurred among them that day, but they will occupy a sacred place in our hearts and in our history. They will never be forgotten.

★ We think about our firefighters and our police officers and our emergency workers as heroes, and they truly are. But I think of all of the people of New York City as heroes.

On being asked by Barbara Walters how he comforts all the children who lost parents in the September 11 attacks:

★ I tell them that nobody can take their daddy from them . . . that their father helped to create them. That all these wonderful things that they're hearing about their dad is in them. So when they hear the eulogies and the explanations of how brave their father was, how dedicated, how many medals he won, how many times he saved people, that they should realize that those qualities are inside them and that they're very special children. Because not everybody has a father that is a great man.

After the World Trade Center attacks, Giuliani thought it best for himself and others to "enjoy ourselves since we are alive and in honor of the people who died, they would want us to enjoy ourselves. They would want us to live life."

★ The families here are entitled to know at least one thing in the tragedy that they're now experiencing, and that is that they're not alone, that as they recognize and deal with the fact that they have lost a loved one, they should also realize that all of America stands behind them in helping to educate their children, keep their homes, and keep their families together.

On Veterans Day 2001, two months after the attacks:

★ It is a day in which all New Yorkers and all Americans now understand—maybe better than ever—what our veterans have done for us.

At the lighting of the Rockefeller Center Christmas tree with First Lady Laura Bush, November 2001:

★ Tonight's tree lighting is a salute to our heroes, our traditions, and to the strength and unity of our nation.

Dedicating the 2001 Thanksgiving Day Parade to the victims and rescuers of the World Trade Center collapse:

★ To all of those courageous people and all the people in uniform, this one's for you.

Giuliani carried the Olympic torch through the streets of New York City in late December 2001 and dedicated it to the emergency personnel who died while saving others on September 11.

★ I carry this flame as a representative of these wonderful people.

4

Reaction to the September 11 Attacks

———————— ★ ————————

★ This week that we just ended is the worst week in the history of the city of New York. It could be one of the worst weeks in the history of America.

★ My mother and father . . . could tell you where they were when Pearl Harbor happened. Everybody's going to be able to tell you where they were when the World Trade Center was attacked.

★ We have met the worst of humanity with the best of humanity.

★ The beautiful part is the way people have helped and supported each other.

From an October 2001 Larry King Live *appearance:*

★ I love this city. It's devastating what's been done to it.

On the enormous death toll of September 11:

★ The number of casualties will be more than any of us can bear ultimately.

★ That's something that we're going to have to deal with today and tomorrow, as people absorb the impact of what's actually happened.

★ Ultimately, when you look back on it, you just say, "God decided who was going to make it and who wasn't." The numbers are staggering. It's impossible to really even comprehend. I think it's going to take years to comprehend the amount of damage that was done to human life.

From a September 17 talk at New York's Central Synagogue:

★ It was New York City's worst week. But it was New York City's best week. We have never been braver. We have never been stronger.

★ And the tragic events of September 11 only proved what I'd said all along—that New York City is the strongest, bravest, best city in the world.

Speaking on October 11, one month after the World Trade Center collapse:

★ The fire is still burning, but from it has emerged a stronger spirit.

★ The attack was intended to break our spirit. It has utterly failed. Our hearts are broken, but they continue to beat, and the spirit of our city has never been stronger.

Some compared the devastation of September 11 to that of the assassination of President Kennedy. Giuliani replied:

★ This drama is a longer one. We don't have a closure, like the funeral that took place for President Kennedy.

Coping with the aftermath of September 11 and the anthrax scare:

★ This is very uncharted territory that everybody is in.

5

"Go About Your Lives"

★

Giuliani encouraged people to continue to visit New York City and enjoy its many offerings.

★ Life goes on. And the life of the city is going on, and the prediction that I made on the first day is proving to be true. The city is stronger than it was last week at this time. We've had the most horrible attack in the history of the city, and we have emerged a stronger city. More united, more united with ourselves, more united with the rest of America.

★ On September 11, New York City suffered the darkest day in our history. It's now up to us to make it its finest hour.

★ Show your confidence. Show you're not afraid. Go to restaurants. Go shopping.

★ If you want to show that we can stand up to these terror-ists, that they can't frighten us, they can't affect us, that Americans are just too tough to be affected by that, well then, come to New York and make that point. Come here. Come here and enjoy it. Great restaurants. The best plays in the world. We've got a team headed for the playoffs and we've got great sports. So you come to New York and make that point.

★ New York City is open. It's open for business.

★ We have tremendous assets here. People should take advantage of them and use them, and the more they do, the faster we're going to send a signal to these cowards who attacked us that they can't stop us. We're stronger than they are, much stronger.

★ Come here and spend some money. Go to a restaurant, take in a Broadway play. The life of the city goes on.

★ If you have friends or family who were planning on com-ing to New York City in the near future, tell them to come now. Not only will they have a great time at our world-renowned restaurants, shops, museums, ballparks, and theaters, but they will be making an important statement that terrorists cannot stop us from being the land of the free and the home of the brave.

★ Come to enjoy our thousands of restaurants and museums and sporting events and shopping and Broadway. But also come to take a stand against terrorism.

★ By going about our daily lives, New Yorkers continue to show the world that we will not give in to fear. We are taking full advantage of the blessings of freedom, and are setting an excellent example of how even in these trying times, we can move ahead.

On the Delta Air Lines decision to give away ten thousand free airline tickets to encourage travel to New York City following September 11:

★ I think it's just a wonderful way to make a statement about the fact that terrorists can't stop us or hinder us from doing what we want by coming to New York City.

Praising attendance at the October 2001 World Series:

★ It's important for the spirit of the city. The fact that all these people showed up unafraid, undeterred, I think it's absolutely terrific.

★ They're not going to stop me from going to a baseball game. Kids have to play ball . . . we're going to prevail.

★ I want to encourage people to make sure they get into the holiday spirit and come shopping in New York City.

The first edition of Saturday Night Live *following September 11 aired September 29, 2001, and featured Rudy Giuliani in a tribute to the World Trade Center victims and heroes. He began the show as it has always begun.*

★ Live, from New York! It's Saturday Night!

★ You've got to go ahead and live your life, and you can't let these people stop us.

★ People should calm down, relax, be brave . . . and go about their lives.

Urging the nation to carry on during an October 2001 Larry King Live *appearance:*

★ Don't let them stop you. You're safe. You're safe as human beings can be.

★ Land of the free and home of the brave. Is that what it says? Land of the free, home of the brave. So let's be brave. Let's get out there and do the things that we're supposed to do.

On New York City's recovery:

★ Maybe some people just don't know it yet. It's better because spiritually it's a stronger place. And people know it better and respect it more.

6

On Terrorism

---- ★ ----

★ If you want to build a society on sound principles, there's no question that you reject terrorism.

In an action later criticized by both the State Department and the United Nations, Giuliani dismissed PLO leader Yasser Arafat from an October 1995 concert at Lincoln Center celebrating the United Nations' fiftieth anniversary and attended by other world leaders. Arafat was not on the guest list and was asked to leave by the mayor's staff.

★ When we're having a party and a celebration, I would rather not have someone who was implicated in the murders of Americans there.

★ I am comfortable with my decision and I am very proud of it. I would not invite Yasser Arafat to anything, anywhere, anytime, anyplace.

★ And if I had a chance to do it all over again, I'd do it exactly the same way. I think we need to be reminded that Yasser Arafat is a murderer and a terrorist.

★ He was not forcibly removed from the concert. He was told he wasn't invited.

★ I don't think we should be unrealistic about who Yasser Arafat is or what he stands for.

★ I don't have any romance about him. Yasser Arafat is a murderer and a terrorist.

★ I have no doubt about that fact that Yasser Arafat has participated in some of the worst terrorist acts of the last twenty or thirty years, having investigated some of them myself as a United States attorney.

Following the July 1996 crash of TWA Flight 800:

★ We've gone through a long period where we've felt it couldn't happen here. And it may be that this wasn't a terrorist incident, and maybe that it was. In any event, I think we should treat it as a wake-up call, and we should be more serious about security. And it means more inconvenience. But what I've found is, people accept it after a period of time. And they understand.

*From the mayor's August 1997 Capitol Hill hearing
testimony before the Subcommittee on Immigration:*

★ Many of the darkest moments in our nation's history have
come as a result of heinous acts of terrorism. . . . Rather than
look the other way, I believe it is the duty of responsible public
officials to do everything in our power to detain dangerous
individuals and prevent them from entering the country.

★ It would seem to me that if you wanted to build a society
on sound principles you would leave no question about the
fact that you reject terrorism, that you turn over every terrorist
that you can find, and you don't leave any ambiguity about
that.

★ This is a free society . . . you want it to stay that way. And
you don't want terrorists to really attain their objective of
destroying freedom and democracy, which they could do if we
overreact.

*From the mayor's "Statement of Principles on the Future
Status of Jerusalem Address," January 2001:*

★ But the reality is that peace has to be based on security. As
agreements and concessions are made, people have to see that
their lives are becoming safer, more secure, more free of terrorism, and more harmonious with law and democracy.

Following the September 11 attacks:

★ This is a vicious, unprovoked act, a horrible attack on
innocent men, women, and children. It's one of the most
heinous acts, certainly, in world history.

★ We need to remain united—as individuals, as Americans, and as countries committed to life in the civilized world—against the tyranny of terrorism.

★ With bullets and bombs and now with hijacked airplanes, terrorists deny the dignity of human life. Terrorism preys particularly on cultures and communities that practice openness and tolerance. Their targeting of innocent civilians mocks the efforts of those who seek to live together in peace as neighbors. It defies the very notion of being a neighbor.

★ There is no excuse for mass murder, just as there is no excuse for genocide.

★ We do not want these cowardly terrorists to have us in any way alter our American way of life. And I'd like New York to demonstrate that to people.

★ This was not just an attack on the city of New York or on the United States of America. It was an attack on the very idea of a free, inclusive, and civil society.

★ We have to eliminate the threat of terrorism.

★ There's always vulnerability in life. You're never going to remove the vulnerability in life. And the reality is that we have to deal with this new phenomenon, this idea of terrorism striking America, which never happened to us before. We have to tighten up our laws. We have to be willing to be more patient for security checks and security checkpoints. We have to do the things that are reasonable and sensible to protect us. . . .

*On Russian president Vladimir Putin's immediate support
of the international coalition against terrorism following
the September 11 attacks:*

★ He said this was a real opportunity for the people of Russia
and the people of the United States to cement a very enduring
friendship. He said that on a smaller scale the people of Russia
have had to deal with terrorism for some time now, but they
have never had to deal with anything of this magnitude and
that the people of Russia have not become used to it but have
learned to factor terrorism into their daily lives and this is
something we are all going to have to do.

*From the mayor's October 2001 "Address to the United
Nations General Assembly on Combating Terrorism."
Giuliani was the first New York mayor to address the UN
General Assembly since 1952.*

★ I ask you to look into your hearts and recognize that there
is no room for neutrality on the issue of terrorism. You're
either with civilization or with terrorists.

★ The United Nations must hold accountable any country
that supports or condones terrorism.

★ There's no room for neutrality here. There's no room for the usual diplomatic on-the-one-hand-but-on-the-other, because this isn't about diplomacy. . . . This is about murder. This is about cold-blooded, vicious, insane murderers. And unless we eliminate them, they're going to kill more people. . . . And all this, all this stuff about you have to understand how they feel, they lost the right to ask us to understand how they feel when they murdered over five thousand people. They lost the right to do that. They no longer have that right. You lose that right when you engage in mass murder of innocent people. It doesn't exist. And if you . . . entertain that right for people, if you entertain the right to get our attention by murdering five thousand innocent people, we're going to have an uncivilized, chaotic world, and our children are going to grow up in a more dangerous world.

★ The best long-term deterrent to terrorism—obviously—is the spread of our principles of freedom, democracy, the rule of law, and respect for human life. The more that spreads around the globe, the safer we will all be. These are very powerful ideas and once they gain a foothold, they cannot be stopped.

★ We are right and they are wrong. It is as simple as that.

★ This is not a time for further study or vague directives. The evidence of terrorism's brutality and inhumanity, of its contempt for life and the concept of peace, is lying beneath the rubble of the World Trade Center less than two miles from where we meet today.

★ Good intentions alone are not enough to conquer evil.

★ Let those who say that we must understand the reasons for terrorism come with me to the thousands of funerals we're having in New York City—thousands—and explain those insane, maniacal reasons to the children who will grow up without fathers and mothers and to the parents who have had their children ripped from them for no reason at all.

On promoting the eradication of terrorism during an October 2001 Larry King Live *appearance:*

★ And then let's prepare a response, as the president is doing, so that we systematically and thoroughly eliminate terrorism—not just deal with this issue, but eliminate terrorism all over the world.

★ We want peace. But you're not going to get to peace by not eliminating terrorism. You're just going to get more destruction, more devastation. What makes the people who are marching for that kind of irrational peace think that they're not going to do this again? These are the same people that thought we'd achieve peace by making concessions to Hitler and appeasing Hitler. And what did that bring? It brought twelve . . . million people dead. If we had faced him at an earlier stage and dealt with him, maybe those people wouldn't have died. . . . I want peace. I think the president wants peace. But I think we maybe have a more mature understanding of how you get to peace. You don't just walk around carrying signs and singing songs and get to peace when there are people that want to murder five thousand people, and maybe they want to murder a lot more than five thousand people.

*Addressing a Jerusalem crowd in an October 2001
telephone call with Mayor Ehud Olmert of Jerusalem:*

★ I am very confident that together we are going to overcome terror.

*From a December 2001 trip to Jerusalem with Mayor-elect
Michael Bloomberg and Governor George E. Pataki of New
York:*

★ The people of Jerusalem and the people of New York City
are shoulder-to-shoulder, and the people of America and the
people of Israel are shoulder-to-shoulder in the fight against
terrorism.

★ The American and Israeli people have to keep going out.
We cannot let the terrorists win.

★ I can think of no other people, no other country, who gave
us more support, who gave us an example of how to stand up
to terror than the people of Israel.

*Giuliani then went on to say his aim is "true peace and not
the romance of peace."*

★ The U.S. and Israel have to stand together for democracy
and the rule of law and against the fanatics who oppose them.

While touring ground zero with Prime Minister Ariel Sharon of Israel in December 2001, Guiliani was asked by a reporter if he regretted his decision to refuse the $10 million check from Saudi Arabian prince Alwaleed Bin Talal Bin AbdulAziz Alsaud after the prince criticized American foreign policy in the Middle East. Giuliani said:

★ You've got to be kidding. No, I'm very proud of it. No way I would take money from someone who was trying to use that as a way of propagating the idea of moral equivalency between democracies and terrorist states. . . . The money was offered to us as an attack on America.

★ There is no moral equivalent to this attack. There is no justification for it. The people who did it lost any right to ask for justification for it when they slaughtered four or five thousand innocent people, and to suggest that there is any justification for it only invites this happening in the future.

From the mayor's Farewell Address, December 2001:

★ Our enemies insanely commit suicide to serve some irrational purpose. And they think that we are afraid—they used to think that we are afraid to die for what we believe in. And the reality is that we don't want to die. And we don't believe that it's our right to make that choice for ourselves. We think God only has that right. But the reality is that we're just a few blocks from a site in which hundreds and hundreds of men and women freely by choice gave up their life. First, to protect the lives of other people. And secondly, to preserve the dignity and honor of the United States of America while under attack.

On the war on terrorism:

★ The war will go on for some time. But I hope you realize we've already won it. We've already won the war. It's just a matter now of finishing it . . . I know we won because I saw within hours the reaction of the people of New York City and the reaction of the people of the United States of America.

★ Yet even as we mourn our dead and prepare for what could be a long and bitter war against an elusive enemy, let us always remember that our greatest national strengths are our openness, our diversity, our inclusiveness, and our freedom.

★ The inherent justice of our nation's war against terrorism becomes only clearer with time.

On Osama bin Laden:

★ This is a very, very evil man.

Reaction to the December 2001 release of videotapes of Osama bin Laden rejoicing in the September 11 massacre:

★ It's the most detailed and chilling description of a premeditated murder that I've ever heard, and I've prosecuted cases that were pretty horrendous, a lot of them. I don't think I've ever heard a description of a person who planned to kill a mass number of people and then delights in the fact that it turns out to be more than he had originally planned.

★ I think if you presented this in court to any jury, the jury wouldn't even leave the jury box.

★ The public has a right to know this, and it does support the necessity for the continued response of the United States and our allies in doing what we have to do to eliminate this form of fanatic ideology.

★ You don't even need this tape to come to the judgment that he's the one responsible for this.

On bin Laden, seen at one point on the videotape laughing about the casualties:

★ It doesn't surprise me that that's the way he feels. . . . Everything I've read about him and knew about him certainly supports the fact that . . . he'd be the kind of person that would delight in doing this . . . it probably indicates now how fiendish he actually is.

★ The sickening video showing Osama bin Laden cheerfully claiming credit for the atrocities of September 11 steels our resolve to prevent this madman and his associates from ever perpetrating another act of terror. This unwavering determination will propel our recovery efforts and embolden us as we seek justice in the name of all those who were so cruelly taken from us.

★ This is one of the most significant things in our history, one of the most significant attacks on America, and we have a right to know . . . as much as we possibly can about why it happened and how it happened. . . . I think it's in the interest of our . . . country to convince any of the doubters that may exist, particularly those who maybe don't support us as wholeheartedly as they should, that this is a dangerous man, an evil man, and a man whose intent is to continue to kill until and unless he's captured.

★ When you consider the fact that this man is gloating over the number of people that died at the World Trade Center, and seems to be happy about the fact that it was more than he says he anticipated, do you need any more to realize that the actions that our government has taken in order to try to find him, in order to try to find the people who support him and help him, and try to eliminate that threat, is perfectly justified as a matter of just plain self-defense?

★ I can't imagine anyone questioning that he's the one responsible for what happened at the World Trade Center. . . .

In support of presidential action to prosecute terrorists involved in the September 11 attacks:

★ And I think what he has to know is that all of us in New York support him, and support him completely, in the efforts that he's going to have to make over the next couple of days, weeks, and to make a point that people can't do this. You can't attack innocent men, women, and children. And ultimately, I am totally confident that American democracy and the American rule of law will prevail, and the people of New York are going to help to demonstrate that over the next couple of days.

7

Rising Above Terror

———————— ★ ————————

★ On September 11, New York City suffered the darkest day in our long history. The destruction of the World Trade Center, and the resulting loss of thousands of lives, has broken our city's heart. But our heart still beats and our city remains strong. We will emerge from this stronger than we have ever been before.

★ I want the people of New York to be an example to the rest of the country and the rest of the world that terrorism can't stop us.

★ As Americans, we need to reassert our fundamental human right to live in freedom from fear. Our nation is strong and united, and now more than ever, we are the land of the free and the home of the brave.

★ Let's not give in to the cowards who committed this despicable act.

★ New York is still here. We've undergone tremendous losses, and we're going to grieve for them horribly, but New York is going to be here tomorrow morning, and it's going to be here forever.

★ Hatred, prejudice, anger, and irrational reaction to things is what caused this terrible tragedy. And people of the city of New York should act differently. We should act bravely. We should act in a tolerant way. We should go about our business, and we should show these people that they can't stop us, and they can't.

★ New York City will be whole again. We are very, very strong people.

★ We're a free country. Let's act like free people.

★ We're going to come out of this stronger than we were before. Emotionally stronger. Politically stronger. Economically stronger.

★ We shouldn't allow these terrorist cowards to affect us and affect our way of life.

★ The proud twin towers that once crowned our famous skyline no longer stand. But our skyline will rise again.

★ The city is going to come out of this stronger and more determined than it ever was before.

★ The people of the city, their spirit is tremendous. . . . This city is the greatest city in the world. It has the greatest people, and a bunch of cowardly terrorists can't make us fearful.

From a September 19, 2001, letter from the mayor's office:

★ Through the days, weeks, and months to come, New York City stands together, our spirit remains confident, and our resolve to emerge even stronger is steadfast.

★ We know we can rebuild, we know we can get stronger.

Giuliani said the terrorists "attempted to break our spirit— instead they have emboldened it."

★ The World Trade Center was one of the great visible symbols of New York. But the real symbol of New York is the spirit of its people.

★ So the thing that we have to do is demonstrate that the spirit of New York City is not just buildings. The buildings are important to us, but the spirit of New York is about the spirit of its people, that we're a free people, that we're dedicated to democracy, and that we're not going to allow these cowards to stop New York from being the greatest city in the world because it is and it's going to continue to be.

★ There's no question we're going to rebuild.

★ We have shown the world that our faith in democracy and the blessings of freedom are unwavering even in the face of the most senseless and brutal of attacks.

★ Democracy's foundation in this country is simply too strong for anyone to shake, and New Yorkers have demonstrated this fact by living their lives in freedom and paying tribute to all of those who risk and have given their lives to defend it.

★ But even as we grieve for our loved ones, it's up to us to face our future with renewed determination. Our hearts are broken, but they are beating, and they are beating stronger than ever. New Yorkers are unified. We will not yield to terrorism. We will not let our decisions be made out of fear. We choose to live our lives in freedom.

★ To those who say the city will never be the same, I say you are right. It will be better.

★ Through our outpouring of support for the recovery and rebuilding efforts and the determination with which we've gone ahead with our lives, we have already shown the world that New Yorkers do not cave in to terror. We are stronger and more united than ever before, and we will continue to move forward, refusing to surrender to fear.

★ We've got to rebuild our buildings. We have to rebuild people's lives. And we have to rebuild our economy.

★ Really, this has inspired New Yorkers to fight back in a way that I think is even more intense than the actual situation. I mean, they're really incredible people.

★ For a quarter century, the World Trade Center stood as the crown jewel of the Manhattan skyline. Through images ingrained in film and television, people in every corner of the world saw the twin towers as a symbol of the American way of life and the spirit of our city. Now our city is facing one of the most difficult challenges in its long history: enduring tremendous losses, rebuilding our spirit, and emerging a stronger city. I know we will meet these challenges; after all, we are New Yorkers, and we are Americans.

★ This generation has exactly the courage of the generation that fought the Second World War. They inherited it. They were taught it. They have it. They're just as strong, and they're just as capable of defending themselves and defending democracy.

★ This is a situation in which New Yorkers do not have to feel like they're alone. It's just the opposite. We've got plenty of help, including plenty of leadership.

When asked by NBC News's Tom Brokaw if New York City could "come back all the way," Giuliani said:

★ It is going to come back better and stronger.

★ We have to end terrorism. I believe the United States government is committed to that, and it's going to require us here in America to go about our way of life and not have them imperil it. And New York should be an example of that since we seem to be, along with the Pentagon in Washington, the first place in which they've attacked us.

★ American democracy is much stronger than a vicious, cowardly terrorist, and we're going to overcome this.

★ We must show we are not afraid. It shows our confidence.

8

At Ground Zero

─────────────── ★ ───────────────

In the days following the attacks, Giuliani toured ground zero—the name given to the World Trade Center wreckage—with numerous national and international leaders.

★ I think they begin to understand that even being neutral about the idea of terrorism is inhumane.

★ Maybe they'll understand what terrorism can do now.

On touring ground zero with President Vladimir Putin:

★ He was like so many others shocked at the extent of the devastation, very upset about it and supportive of the United States and what we need to do to defend ourselves against terrorism.

On touring ground zero with daughter, Caroline:

★ She wanted to see it. She was upset but not overwrought. It's my job to do for my kids what my father did for me—try to help them figure out how to deal with fear. How to live life, even though you are afraid.

After touring the site with others, Giuliani took some time to view the destruction himself.

★ I'd taken so many people down there with cameras, I just wanted to walk by myself through there and see it and feel it and talk to people.

Reaction to the site where the World Trade Center once stood:

★ The enormity of it hits you, and you just start to cry. Just when you think you've processed it all you realize what they did.

★ When I look at the exposed walls and the vastness of it all and I remember what was there before, I still can't believe that this happened in the modern world, in America—in New York City.

★ Every time you go down there and you look at the site, you're filled with a sense of horror and anger that someone could do this.

★ I don't think I've come down here without a very, very strong emotional reaction to the horror of what the terrorists did to us.

★ When you see it . . . something different happens. It's a different experience. You stand there thinking, "How can it be? How can it be? How could they do this?"

★ It is impossible to actually convey your impressions when you're actually there and you actually see it. It's hard to believe that this is actually real. It seems like it must be a nightmare or it must be some movie that you're watching.

★ I do believe there is something very, very different that happens when you actually get to see it. I think that all of the pictures on television, all the photographs that you can take of it, say one thing, actually seeing it says another.

★ I've never seen anything like that in my whole life. I suspect no one else has. The destruction is enormous. The debris is beyond any description.

★ When you see it from the air, you realize how devastating it is, how massive. I think seeing that smoke come out, it just makes you angry, and it makes you determined.

On reconstruction of the World Trade Center:

★ There should be a memorial here for the massive number of people that we lost. There should be a memorial here to the spirit of America that's going to rebuild it.

★ It's hallowed ground, it's special ground. It's a burial ground, a resting place for some of the bravest people that existed in our country.

★ It has to be a beautiful, inspirational memorial because we have now to accept the fact that it is going to be the burial ground for many, many people.

★ I really believe we shouldn't think about this site out there, right behind us, right here, as a site for economic development. We should think about a soaring, monumental, beautiful memorial that just draws millions of people here that just want to see it.

★ We should think about how we can find the most creative minds possible who love and honor Americans and can express that.

During his Farewell Address, Giuliani restated the sacred nature and significance of the ground where the World Trade Center once stood.

★ Long after we are all gone, it's the sacrifice of our patriots and their heroism that is going to be what this place is remembered for. This is going to be a place that is remembered one hundred and one thousand years from now, like the great battlefields of Europe and of the United States. And we really have to be able to do with it what they did with Normandy or Valley Forge or Bunker Hill or Gettysburg. We have to be able to create something here that enshrines this forever and that allows people to build on it and grow from it.

★ Their families need to be protected just as if they had been alive. This place has to be sanctified. It has to become a place, when anybody comes, that they immediately feel the power, strength, and emotion of what it means to become an American. . . . This is too important a place.

On the public's visits to ground zero:

★ And they're coming for all of the best of reasons. They're coming because they care, they're coming because they're traumatized, they're coming because they believe they can be helpful. . . .

At the December 2001 opening of public viewing platforms surrounding the World Trade Center wreckage:

★ There is an undeniable need to witness in person the site of the most horrible attack on our nation in history. These platforms will provide a vantage point to do that while fully respecting the solemnity of this place.

★ People from all over the world want to come here for I think the most appropriate of reasons . . . They realize something very horrendous and something very magnificent happened here. It's going to be part of our history forever.

★ I really urge Americans to come here and say a little prayer and reflect on the whole history of America.

★ It is hallowed ground. It is sacred ground. So we decided to put these platforms because there has been so much interest in seeing this site. Hopefully, doing it will accomplish a lot of different purposes. It will accomplish the purpose of allowing people to observe this site of horror, this site of great bravery. It will allow people to reflect on the importance of human life. It will allow people to reflect on the importance of democracy and political freedom.

PART II

GIULIANI ON GIULIANI

———— ★ ————

9

Giuliani Himself

———————— ★ ————————

★ I enjoy myself, I enjoy life. I love comedy. I love opera. I love music. I love baseball.

★ The reason I'm such a fortunate man is that I have people that love me and I love them, and they care for me and I care for them. And that's the greatest support that you can have in life.

Larry King once asked Giuliani how he sees himself:

★ I see myself as me. . . . I'm a direct person. I tell you what I think. I'm an honest person. And I just see myself as me. And then everybody else has to figure out what my image is.

★ I would admit that I am a maverick, yes, and I'm an independent, a reformer.

★ I had this youthful conviction that all human beings were basically good. If you just turned on the right switch, goodness and rationality would flow forth. I came to realize that rationality does not necessarily rule and that some people were simply evil. There was very little you could do to change them, and if you entertained the romantic notion that they could be changed, you would wind up endangering innocent people.

★ What I don't allow to happen is, I don't allow other people to determine my view of myself. I have a pretty solid idea of what I'm doing, and why I'm doing it.

On being compared to former U.S. attorney and presidential candidate Thomas Dewey:

★ Somebody once asked me if I see Tom Dewey's face in the mirror when I wake up. No—and I am not sure I want to.

★ I try to demand good performance out of myself, although not perfection. I know you make mistakes.

★ I just try to be myself. I do the best that I can being straight with people, being myself.

★ I have a pretty good sense that I'm very, very human, that I make a lot of mistakes, and that I got to keep working on it. And if I don't, my mother reminds me of it all the time.

★ I pride myself in displaying good judgment about people.

★ Sometimes I can be very excitable. I am Italian, after all!

★ And I'm a big optimist, and generally look at things, almost everything, from the positive point of view. And I don't think you can get through life if you don't look at everything, no matter how difficult it is, from a positive point of view.

On his path to becoming a Republican:

★ I was a Democrat, an Independent, and then I became a Republican, so I had a real transformation.

★ The things I do not accept without response is when somebody tries to impugn your integrity.

★ I'm very tough but not difficult to get along with. And I'm very reasonable.

★ I've lived in New York City all of my life. I was born there, I've gone to school there, I've been elected.

★ I'm familiar with enough places to know that this is a city so filled with promise, with good people and great opportunity, that I truly cannot picture living anywhere else.

On being asked by CNN's Bernard Shaw about his "famous temper," December 1993:

★ And my temper maybe is overdone. I have a real commitment to working hard and to getting people around me to work hard and sometimes, sometimes in order to motivate people, maybe I'm a little stronger than I should be. But that's the desire. It really isn't temper.

Talk show host Oprah Winfrey interviewed Giuliani in her January 2002 issue of The Oprah Magazine, *in which she asked the mayor how he dealt with the times when people were "unkind" to him.*

★ You have to keep a strong sense of who you really are— and I have a pretty strong sense of myself. It gets me in trouble when I say this, but I don't think of myself as a politician. I've always tried to be honest when communicating with people.

While learning to in-line skate with son Andrew in 1994:

★ I do it quietly. I do it at night. I do it so nobody can watch me.

On being asked by NBC national correspondent Jamie Gangel if he's bothered when people call him "mean":

★ I guess sometimes. . . . I think they would like a different me, which is the politically correct caricature they've created of what an American politician is like. And then when an American politician is like that, they hate him for being that way.

★ I don't get offended any longer when people call me crazy. . . .

★ I take a different view of someone comparing me to Adolf Hitler than when someone calls me a jerk.

On his love of opera:

★ Probably, it's genetic. I think if you're Italian, there has to be an interest in opera. It just is in your chromosomes.

Giuliani once said opera "gives you a wonderful feeling, a real sense of having captured the universe."

As a youth with a new love of classical music and opera, Giuliani recalls buying George Frideric Handel's opera Julius Caesar.

★ I saw a *Julius Caesar* album for ninety-eight cents. I followed the opera by reading the libretto printed on the back of the album jacket. I fell in love with the record. It was like a revelation.

★ I was in Klein's department store on a Saturday afternoon, looking for a popular record. I had a certain number of rock 'n' roll records, and I wandered off to the classical section and bought three records at once: Handel's *Julius Caesar*, Verdi's *La Traviata*, and the *1812 Overture*. And I went home and played them and fell in love.

On rediscovering the joys of golf:

★ I was wrong. I'd never give it up again, and I regret having neglected it for twenty-five years.

★ Golf takes a lot of time, but that's what relaxes me. Playing convinces you that life can be about something besides work. I was dead wrong about this crazy game.

★ What's funny, though, is that usually dads get their sons into golf. It was the other way around with Andrew and me.

*In June 2001, Giuliani's son, Andrew, joined golf
professional Tiger Woods for a round at the Buick Open:*

★ That was . . . an overwhelming experience. On the first tee,
after Tiger Woods teed off with the great shots that he always
hit, when Andrew got ready to tee off—I have to be truthful—
I closed my eyes. I just said a little prayer. And I knew if it were
me, I would have been shaking so bad I wouldn't have been
able to sling the driver. But he played really, really well, and
he's a great kid. And Tiger Woods is a wonderful man for the
generous and kind way in which he treated him and everybody
else.

On his children:

★ My kids are remarkable. We have a very good
relationship. . . .

10

The Giuliani Humor

─────────── ★ ───────────

★ Haven't you seen my act? I already play a Republican playing a Democrat playing a Republican.

Talking to Larry King about death threats received while prosecuting the Mafia:

★ When I came into office, my first big mob case, one of the people involved in it put out a contract to kill me for $400,000. And it was serious. And they caught the person who was involved in it, they prosecuted him, and it got all resolved. Then in the last year I was in office . . . one of the same groups put out a contract on my life for only $200,000. . . . I'm worth at least $800,000, come on.

*Less than twenty-four hours after winning the 1993
election, Giuliani appeared as himself on the popular
sitcom* Seinfeld. *In a scene demonstrating his real-life
commitment to New Yorkers and ridding the city of
corruption, the mayor-elect vowed to investigate the alleged
misrepresentation of the fat content of frozen yogurt
products.*

★ My campaign staff has received some very disturbing
information regarding the fat content in yogurt that's being
sold throughout the city. I pledge to you now that if I'm
elected mayor, as my first order of business, I'll appoint a special task force to investigate this matter. I promise you, my fellow New Yorkers, that Mayor Giuliani will do everything possible to cleanse the city of this falsified nonfat yogurt.

*Joking with David Letterman about his son's antics during
the inauguration:*

★ The night before, we had gone over the notes together,
so . . . Andrew had done this many times during the campaign.
He would get up and give a speech with me. So when I stood
up, he thought, "Well, it's time for me to stand up, too."

*On the ability of his nemesis, Public Advocate Mark Green,
to attract the press:*

★ New York is the best place to be on a slow news day. Just
ask Mark Green.

*On his likeness in wax at Madam Tussaud's Wax Museum,
April 2000:*

★ He looks better than me. I think they made it a flattering
version. He seems to smile more.

On Hillary Rodham Clinton's run for New York Senator:

★ I'm looking forward to see what kind of support I can get, and also to see the fun we could have as I travel to Arkansas and announce that although I've never lived there, never worked there, and don't know much about the place, I'm running for the Senate.

Two weeks after the September 11 attacks, Rudy Giuliani and other emergency personnel appeared on New York City's Saturday Night Live, *praising the heroes of the attacks and urging the city to get back to business. "Can we be funny?" asked the executive producer, Lorne Michaels. "Why start now?" quipped Giuliani.*

The mayor delivered the popular Top 10 "Things I Will Miss About Being Mayor" during a November 2001 appearance on the Late Show *with David Letterman:*

★ 10. If I feel like sleeping in, I call a citywide snow emergency.

   9. Naming a street after someone is a great, inexpensive Christmas gift.

   8. If I want tickets to *The Producers,* I just pick up the phone and, four or five months later, I get tickets.

   7. The look on people's faces when they realize the key to the city doesn't open a damn thing.

   6. I'm double-parked right now. Who's gonna tow me?

   5. That smell in the subway. Call me crazy, but I've grown to love it.

   4. When someone catches a 'gator in Central Park, guess who gets to keep it.

3. Street vendors sell me counterfeit DVDs, half-price.

2. The New York Yankees winning all those World Series? That was my idea.

1. The daily call from Letterman, begging me to reopen strip clubs.

In his final appearance on New York's Saturday Night Live, *Giuliani and "Weekend Update" hosts Tina Fey and Jimmy Fallon sang, "Will You Still Love Me Tomorrow?" to an emotional audience not yet ready to say good-bye to their mayor. After Fey asked if he really had to leave office, Giuliani replied:*

★ Yes, I do. And you can't come with me.

Giuliani appeared on the Late Show *with David Letterman for a final time as mayor on December 27, 2001. He had been a guest over twenty times while in office. When asked if he thought "things would be different after September 11" had Al Gore been elected president, Giuliani replied:*

★ You're asking someone who, while I was going through radiation, volunteered to go down to Florida to campaign for George W. Bush.

Letterman then asked Giuliani if would earn "big fees" for his work as a consultant.

★ I should hope so. After all, I'm not a communist.

11

The Early Years

★

A lifelong New Yorker, Rudolph William Louis Giuliani was the only child of Helen and Harold Giuliani, born May 28, 1944, in Brooklyn, New York.

★ I believe, because my father and mother taught me this, that you should be honest with people.

★ I really have followed this all my life . . . maybe my father taught me this . . . Do the job you have in front of you. If you do a good job of it, you have a future, if you don't, then you don't have a future doing much of anything.

Giuliani's father served a jail sentence for robbing a milkman at gunpoint in 1934.

★ My father also had to overcome the disappointment that he gave to his father in the mistakes that he made in his life. And he made sure that I wouldn't make the same mistakes. And for that I thank him forever.

★ My father compensated through me. In a very exaggerated way, he made sure that I didn't repeat his mistakes in my life— which I thank him for, because it worked out.

Remembering his father, who died in 1981:

★ My father gave me such a great gift. He gave me an internal sense of how to find a positive way to deal with whatever life has in store for you. But I lost a great source of strength when he died.

★ He worked nights, too, and I didn't see him as much as I'd have liked, but the time I did see him, he had a big impact on me.

★ My father used to have this expression, which was that he didn't want me to love him, he wanted me to respect him. After I respected him, I would learn to love him.

★ My dad taught me a lot of really good things, and he was a wonderful man, but, as I've told . . . my son, daughter, no father is perfect. . . . Fathers make mistakes and fathers are human beings, and I tend to think now that love is more important than I thought it was.

In 1999, Giuliani remembered how his father delighted in filing income taxes because he "used to say it's a small price to pay for the freedom that you have in America, and that people should stop complaining about that."

★ My mother wasn't able to get a college education because she had to work to support a family during the depression. So she made sure that she instilled in me a tremendous love of history and reading and a tremendous thirst for learning new things and the excitement of it. It's a great gift that she gave me and it probably came out of the fact that she was deprived of being able to have the fulfillment of the education that she wanted.

★ For my energy, I am very thankful to my mother.

Remembering his grandfather at a 2001 Naturalization Ceremony on Ellis Island with President George W. Bush:

★ As I stand here I think of my grandfather Rodolfo, for whom I'm named, who left Genoa sometime in the latter part of the nineteenth century. I imagine him sitting on the shore of Genoa with his little bag. He only had twenty dollars in his pocket—I got that information from the records of Ellis Island. . . . Excuse me if I say that I am sure he was saying, "I'm coming to the place where the streets are paved with gold—New York City." He found out, of course, that the streets weren't paved with gold, but they were lined with opportunity.

Remembering a firefighting uncle who was injured in the line of duty:

★ My mother would take me to visit him almost every day at Kings County Hospital. He was in tremendous pain, but one of my earliest memories was his talking about wanting to go back to work. It was the thing that got him through, the thing that sustained him. He would talk about how he loved his job. And even as a five- and six-year-old, I could figure it out. Here was a man who had broken both of his legs and maybe his back, and he wanted to go back to the work he loved. And he did. And he was one of my early heroes.

★ I used to come to Coney Island with my grandmother four or five times a year every summer. It was like one of the great outings of the year.

12

Influences and Mentors

———————— ★ ————————

★ From the time I was very young, bravery and courage inspired me. My father had great physical courage. He had been a boxer. I read John Kennedy's *Profiles in Courage* when I was young. My Uncle Rudy, my father's youngest brother, was a police officer for twenty-four years. My mother's second-youngest brother, Edward, was a captain in the fire department, decorated four or five times. She had three other brothers who were police officers. So I grew up with uniforms all around me and their stories of heroism.

★ My father was the finest man I ever knew. He taught me the lesson of being honest.

Giuliani's calm and determined manner, taught by his father, helped New Yorkers during the September 11 attacks.

★ My father used to tell me that in times of crisis, the most important thing, if you want to be helpful, is to remain calm and to actually become calmer as things around you are getting more and more out of control.

Giuliani remembers that the last conversation he had with his father "was about courage and fear. I said to him, 'Were you ever afraid of anything?' He said to me, 'Always.' He said, 'Courage is being afraid but then doing what you have to do anyway.' "

Remembering Brother Jack O'Leary, a high school teacher and early mentor:

★ He was terrific. He spent a lot of time with me, developing interests that I had that I wasn't comfortable about. Like reading and opera, things that I wouldn't talk to my friends about, because they would think I was a sissy.

On the influence of Lloyd F. MacMahon, chief judge of the Southern District of New York appointed by President Eisenhower in 1959, for whom Giuliani clerked after graduating from New York University Law School in 1968:

★ Judge MacMahon, as a teacher, was one of the four or five people who had the biggest impact on my life. He would sit down and patiently explain to me the mistakes that were being made by lawyers who appeared before him. It was practical advice you could never get in law school.

On Robert Kennedy:

★ I thought Robert Kennedy's presence in national politics was irreplaceable. He had the support of the minority community in a way no other white politician did, and he had the ability to communicate with the white middle class. There was no one else with a foot in both camps.

Giuliani once deemed Robert Kennedy "great and brilliant."

On Deputy Attorney General Harold Tyler:

★ Tyler was very good under pressure. I learned from him that in a pressure situation, the best thing to do was remain calmer than everybody else.

From a 1997 Martin Luther King Jr. birthday ceremony:

★ Dr. King didn't expect miracles. But he did expect progress. He did expect each of us to do our part to make the world a better place.

Speaking in April 1999 at Joe DiMaggio's memorial service:

★ The greats often make things look easy. But of course, the struggle is constant.

In 1981, President Reagan appointed Giuliani associate attorney general, the number three position in the Department of Justice. From the Reagan Lecture, Ronald Reagan Presidential Library, September 30, 1999:

★ I was twice given the opportunity by Ronald Reagan to serve my country. Both times I was very, very honored to do it. And it had a lot to do with my formation as a public official, the formation of my thinking, the ideas that I have and the things that I've put into place.

★ The whole history of the world was changed by Ronald Reagan's being willing to stick to his principles and not do what a lesser president or a lesser man might do.

★ I was part of the Reagan administration, and have to this day enormous respect for President Reagan. I think he was a president that uplifted the office . . . I worked for him for two and a half years, and it did a lot to form my political thinking . . . also the way that I manage and run things.

On former first lady Nancy Reagan:

★ She's a great lady and a great American.

Remembering John Cardinal O'Connor, archbishop of New York:

★ He was the most public of religious figures. But he shone just as brightly in private.

★ He healed bodies, as well as souls.

On former New York City mayor John V. Lindsay:

★ John Lindsay defined an era in the life of New York City. . . . John Lindsay's legacy will continue to be debated in the civic discussions that he loved so well. But let the record show that . . . John Lindsay refused to give up on cities when others were abandoning them. He was determined to fashion a new kind of politics that reflected the unique and diverse spirit of the greatest city on earth. He was independent. He was outspoken. He was a reformer. But most of all, he was a New Yorker.

★ He made working for the city seem more altruistic, more idealistic, more exciting than ever before. He lifted my view of what working in government could do for the city of New York.

★ One piece of advice he could give me from his own experience is don't think about any other office. Just do the one you're doing. Do it like you'd be a one-term mayor and then you'll be a two-term mayor.

Praising former New York City mayor John V. Lindsay's reaction to the assassination of Dr. Martin Luther King Jr.:

★ While cities across the nation were exploding in flames, New York remained calm. This was in large part due to the example John Lindsay set, walking the streets late into the night, reaching out to those in pain, and calling for unity and understanding, even in the depths of that terrible time.

PART III

GIULIANI ON POLITICS

★

13

On Being Mayor

———————— ★ ————————

★ This is a very tough job. . . . If you're going to do this job well, or at least you hope you do it well, I think you have to make a lot of tough decisions, and people expect a lot of you, and they get very angry at you when you don't agree with them.

★ I'm never going to have a better job.

★ It's been said that I'm the biggest cheerleader for the city, and it's true. I love New York. I'm very proud to be a New Yorker, and I am honored that the people of this great city have chosen me to be their mayor.

★ I think the more ticker-tape parades I can have during the time that I'm mayor, the more great memories I'm going to have later on.

★ If you look at the way I function and do my job, I haven't missed a beat, probably never will until the day I die.

★ I think that one of the things that I've always done is be able to focus tremendous attention on my job. I love this job. . . . I do it with all my heart and soul. I don't think there's anybody that even questions that.

★ I always much preferred to be referred to as Rudy than either Mayor Giuliani or Giuliani. . . . You have to have a personal relationship with the people of the city, even when they're angry at you.

★ I don't care about people as minorities, or as majorities or as subgroups. I care about people as people. I think the thing wrong with this city is people cared about people as members of subgroups: Italian Americans, Irish Americans, African Americans, this American, that kind of American, some other kind of American. I try very, very hard to care about New Yorkers as New Yorkers.

In 1998, on being popular:

★ I care about being effective. I care about being respected, and I care about history. There are times in which I realize that I'll be unpopular for something that I'm doing. But if I thought about it, and we've analyzed it, and I have confidence that five years from now this is the right direction to go in, then I will stick with it.

★ You've got to stand for something, at least in this city. Otherwise, it rolls all over you.

★ You will always find a large percentage of New Yorkers who disagree with anything that you do or disagree with any aspect of your personality, but the reality is that in the last poll, a majority of New Yorkers actually thought that I was a nice guy and I agree with that majority.

★ What I've learned is, if the mayor shows up, everything happens much more efficiently. Everybody pays a lot more attention. Everything gets much better organized.

★ I think I'm very compassionate. In fact, I think I'm probably more compassionate in a direct sense than most people that have had this job.

★ I know how to do economic development. New York City has a record number of jobs since I've been mayor.

★ This is an enormously demanding job, and your energy has to be applied to doing this job as well as you can do it.

★ I was born here, I grew up here, it's sort of in my blood.

★ If, when my life is over—hopefully a long time from now—and I look back on it and I've had the opportunity to be mayor of New York City for one or two terms, and I had the opportunity to do for the city the things that I wanted to do, that's a very fulfilling life.

★ I am the mayor of the most complex city in the United States.

★ I think that to be mayor of this city, and to do it at all effectively, you have to have a love affair with the people of this city. And I do.

★ I love the people of the city of New York. Some of them love me and some of them hate me, but I think they all have a reaction to me.

★ This administration is a work in progress just as the city itself is a work in progress.

★ I don't feel that my first loyalty is to a political party. I feel that my first loyalty is to the people of the city of New York.

★ I'm always hopeful and optimistic; you have to be if you're the mayor of New York City. . . .

On being sked by Larry King if being mayor of New York City is "as tough as we would imagine":

★ Some days it isn't, some days it is.

★ It's a tough job. . . . It's a job in which everything is right in your face. You have to decide things immediately. And every day you lose a constituency—maybe you gain one, but you'll lose one. But you got to be willing to make decisions. And I think one of the ways in which I've helped turn the city around is I do make decisions and I'm not afraid of controversy if I believe this is the right direction for the city.

★ I know—because this is the great asset that the mayor of New York City always has, which if you understand it, is the key to all success: We may have some of the biggest problems in the world, because we're such a large city. But we have more talent in this city than anyplace else. There's just no question about that. And a sensible government, a rational academic community, and focused businesses working together can accomplish a tremendous amount.

★ In some ways this is the hardest city to run. But in some ways it's the easiest if you do the fundamentals right.

★ I think what I am is very passionate. I take the job very seriously.

14

The Media

───────── ★ ─────────

★ Why are there no term limits on journalists?

★ The prying that goes on into private lives doesn't really add very much to the decisions that you make about people. How is a person doing their job? Are they doing it effectively? Aren't they? What's going on in their private life? In their marriage? I think actually, we have gone way too far in that regard. . . . Or if he's having a health problem of some kind in which he needs some help or he needs some treatment, the question is the same thing: Can he do his job? Can she do her job? Can she function?

On his relationship with the media, 2001:

★ I have two or three press conferences a day, so I have gotten to the point where there's no question that surprises me any longer.

On the private lives of public figures:

★ Things happen to mayors like happen to anyone else.

★ Even a public official, even a public figure, retains some degree of privacy rights, and people should respect that.

★ I think what we want to do is to maintain our privacy and to basically say, "There's a public part to your life and there's a private part to your life, and the private part to my life belongs to me."

★ I'm in public life. I struggle with this all the time. I want to retain some of my privacy. I can't stand how it's ripped away from you the way it is. Some of it's relevant to your job. A lot of it isn't. A lot of it's just voyeurism.

★ I try to leave my private life as private as I'm capable of doing in this job, because I think that the invasions into the private lives of elected and appointed officials don't really help very much in figuring out what kind of job they're doing.

In May 2001, on the media's coverage of his personal life:

★ I think the newspapers, particularly the tabloids, but also the television stations and radio stations should move on.

To overly inquisitive journalists:

★ I actually think you'd feel better about yourself if you didn't ask that question.

★ Well, the answer to all those questions is, my private life is my private life, and you don't have any right to ask me about it.

Rudy and the reporters:

★ Remember the rules: You ask the questions. I say, "No comment."

★ Let's stop being stupid. I mean, really, really stupid. I mean, the level sometimes of questions is at the point of idiocy.

After the media's twist on his comments about a contract to have New York City garbage sent to Virginia:

★ I learned a long time ago in this business not to get spun into being offended by the media when somebody didn't say or intend what it is you're being spun around by.

On tabloids:

★ I think it's damaging because I think it drives some good people away. You really have to develop a very thick skin; after a while you do but there are some people that don't want to go through having to develop that kind of thick skin.

On his personal life:

★ My personal life is my personal life.

★ My relationship with Judith Nathan is an adult one, it's a mature one, it's one that's gone on for two years and I hope it's going to go on forever.

★ And there are people who are voyeurs, and they use that as an excuse to kind of invade the private lives of public people. Yes, they have a right to do it. Is it in good taste to do it? I think most Americans think it probably isn't.

Giuliani spoke with MSNBC's Andrea Mitchell in May 2000 at a nationally broadcast town hall meeting, where he was asked by one attendee how others could look up to him as a leader following several controversial revelations about his personal life.

★ I guess I would just ask people to take a look at me as a human being. I'm not a religious leader . . . I'm a governmental leader, and it's my public records and my public actions and the things that I do as the mayor that you should mostly be concerned about, and your moral concerns . . . should be with your own private life.

On his security detail, May 2000:

★ I'm protected all the time. If I go visit any friends or I go to a ball game, which I do a lot, I have to have a security detail. That's because I'm a person against whom there are threats, both from my job as mayor and from the time that I was U.S. attorney. . . . Believe me, I would prefer to have considerably more privacy in my life. And if anybody thinks that it's nice . . . to be in a situation where you have to be guarded—of course it isn't. . . . It gives you extra attention in your life, and people who do it for me do it brilliantly, they do it terrifically, but I think most people, after a short while, would prefer somewhat more privacy in their life.

15

Politics, Pure and Simple

———————— ★ ————————

★ Politics is politics, and it's important. . . . Life is life and then politics comes somewhere third or fourth or fifth in any person's life who has their priorities straight.

★ Public office is temporary. Love and relationships with people and being able to pursue the things that you really, really enjoy is what is really important in life.

On the life of a politician:

★ You have to be ready for anything.

★ Do your job as best you can. If you succeed at it, you have a great future. If you fail at it, you have no future.

★ Governor Pataki told me once a long time ago that your real friends are the friends that will love and care about you after you're the mayor, the governor, the senator, or the president, and I have some friends like that, and I'm a very fortunate man.

★ What you've got to do to win an election is get people to ask the right questions that end with you as the answer.

On politics in New York City:

★ New York City should be a city in which people run it for the good of the city, not for the good of a political party.

In 1987, Giuliani said New York City politics is "overwhelmed with people seeking what they can grab for themselves."

★ I enjoy politics. I wouldn't be in it if I didn't.

Giuliani once again found himself the talk of the town after announcing his endorsement of New York State governor Mario Cuomo, a Democrat, for reelection in 1994. Republican candidate George Pataki went on to win the election.

★ When I ran for mayor last year, I said that, although I'd most often support Republicans, I would occasionally support Democrats, because, for the good of the city, it is sometimes necessary to support a Democrat who would be much better for this city, this region, and this state than a Republican.

★ I am well aware of the risk that I take as a Republican mayor endorsing a Democratic governor, but I've concluded that the risk is worth taking.

★ A lot of people would say, "The devil made me do it." But, I can't blame the devil. I did it myself.

Giuliani remained committed to his decision to back Cuomo:

★ Don't succumb to the feeling that you can't make a difference. And please don't succumb to the notion that politics cannot change.

On mayoral candidate Fernando Ferrer's claim that Giuliani failed as a moral leader, 1997:

★ It really tells you something about a candidate when they start attacking your morality.

★ New Yorkers like—and they should—mayors who are willing to put the interests of the city ahead of partisan politics.

In August 2000, on Vice President Al Gore's selection of Senator Joseph Lieberman, an Orthodox Jew, as his running mate:

★ It says that no matter what religion, no matter what background, we're all qualified, or not qualified to be president or vice president of the United States. It has nothing to do with religion. And I think . . . in that sense, this will help Al Gore. I think this will help more than it will hurt. And I think we also have to recognize the fact that in some places, unfortunately, it will hurt. There are people that still harbor prejudices, but maybe this can help overcome that.

On pandering:

★ I hate pandering . . . have all my life. It's one of the worst characteristics that politicians have, pandering to people. . . . There's a dishonesty in that that really offends me.

On campaign contributions, June 2001:

★ I conduct myself honestly. I conduct myself honorably. I am very, very careful about making sure that I comply with all those rules and regulations.

Giuliani stressed from the onset of his political career that he was against patronage.

★ From the day that I started exploring running for mayor, I have made it clear to every political leader almost from the first discussion we have had that there will be no jobs or patronage—only decisions made on merit.

★ No deals for jobs, no deals for contributors. What you see is what you get.

★ There will be no patronage in my administration. Not under this mayor's nose.

On political corruption:

★ I don't think there's anybody much worse than a public official who sells his office, except maybe for a murderer.

★ Corruption, unfortunately, goes along too often with American politics. It has no relationship to black or white. It sometimes has a relationship to who is in power at the time.

★ It's generally my rule as an observer of government that you should not remain in office for too long.

★ I think that where political power remains in somebody's hands for a very long period of time, it's the rare individual who doesn't become personally corrupt.

★ People say politics is too dishonest for me. I don't accept their premise that politics is too dishonest or has to be dishonest. If it is, we should change it, because it is screwing people, mostly poor people and little people.

★ I think I can reasonably negotiate with anybody over anything but not in a way that is unethical or unprincipled. I don't think anybody in government should be asked to do that.

After his assistant attorney Daniel N. Perlmutter pleaded guilty to stealing evidence from a case—over $450,000 worth of heroin and cocaine—from an office safe, in 1985:

★ The first thing we have to realize is we have to investigate ourselves. We have to aggressively investigate agents, police officers, assistant U.S. attorneys. We're in a dangerous business, and that's one of the prices you pay.

★ It was like a death in the family. He is someone I trusted. He all of a sudden became a suspect and a defendant like everyone else you investigate.

*On the 1986 prosecution of Bronx Democratic leader
Stanley Friedman, who, with a New York businessman and
two former city officials, was found guilty of political
corruption:*

★ This verdict is a very significant victory for the honest and
decent citizens of New York City who have had to labor under
the yoke of people like Stanley Friedman for too darn long,
crooked politicians and crooked bosses of political organiza-
tions that are running counties that are in dire need of honest,
decent people running those counties, who are raping those
counties for their own advantage.

Giuliani's views of public office during the Friedman trial:

★ During the investigation and the trial, I really got the sense
that the political situation . . . was pretty disgusting. You have
to deal with a group of people that I just don't want to spend
any time with. . . . They're essentially the kinds of people that
I've spent most of my life investigating and trying to put in
prison. And it's hard to think of having to spend a lot of time
with them in professional endeavors.

★ I prefer to be with decent people, rather than the kinds of
people that infest New York politics.

*Speaking as United States attorney for the Southern
District of New York in 1986 on attempts to restore ethics
to NYC politics:*

★ Nothing is greater than the will of the electorate, not even
the power of the bribe.

★ There are people who disagree, but my philosophy is a philosophy of returning power to people, and removing some of that power from government.

★ I don't use as my guide public opinion polls and political spinning. I use as my guide the sense that I have of the right principles that you should advocate for.

From the 1999 Manhattan Institute Conference, "The New Urban Paradigm":

★ Accountability replaces unmanageability. Accountability basically says a city is no more difficult to run than any organization. Every organization is difficult to run. Every organization has difficulties in getting to the precise goal that is intended for it, but that doesn't make them unmanageable. It means you have to be accountable, you have to be honest, you have to lay out what you can achieve, and then try to proceed in order to accomplish that. And in doing that you rebuild people's confidence in government.

On leadership:

★ Leadership is not about polls.

★ Sometimes leadership means taking unpopular positions . . . rejecting harmful political fads . . . sometimes leadership requires challenging myths.

★ Leadership is more important than systems, plans, or strategies.

★ You lead by example, or you really don't lead.

On the presidency:

On being asked by CNN correspondent Gene Randall in August 1997 if he would like to be president of the United States:

★ No, I'd like to be mayor of New York City. This is the capital of the world. I have actually told Governor Pataki that I concede that Albany is the capital of New York State, and I've told President Clinton that I concede that Washington is the capital of the United States. But New York City is the capital of the world. So I've got a great job, and I'm hoping that I'll hold on to it.

On being asked in 1998 by NBC national correspondent Jamie Gangel if he has "always wanted to be president":

★ No, I haven't always wanted to be president . . . I think it's a very daunting—it's almost something that I don't like to talk about. . . . there's like a sacredness to it that you shouldn't really talk about it unless at some point in your life you decide to do it, and then you should do it. . . . I don't give it a great deal of thought. It seems like a very remote kind of thing.

On the 2000 presidential election:

★ I think the difference between whether we are going to challenge ourselves to much higher ideals and values over the next several years really depends on whether we have a good chance of electing a Republican president in the year 2000.

★ I think ultimately it's going to be a close election, but I think George W. Bush is going to win. And I think if he keeps emphasizing his record in Texas as a governor, as a leader, and if he gets the issues on education where he's had a superb record in improving the educational performance in Texas more than most other states, then I think he'll win.

On the eve of President Clinton's last day in office, January 2001:

★ I was thinking about him last night. . . . We walked past the White House, took a look at it, and I was thinking, well, it has to be a sad night, no matter what, as you come to the end of your term. But, in a certain way, it's actually easier for him, as it will be for me. You weren't voted out of office, all right. You're leaving on your own power and as—by operation of law—so I think, actually, that's a little bit easier than if he'd been voted out of office.

In January 2001, on the eve of the inauguration of President George W. Bush:

★ We're going to have a grand inauguration tomorrow, a new president, a chance for America to reinvent itself under George W. Bush.

Referring to Republican conservatives and others, October 1999:

★ And I just hope they remember that at the end of the day, we want a Republican president in the year 2000. We don't want to continue this Clinton administration in any form.

On former vice president and presidential candidate Al Gore:

★ I don't think anybody looks at Al Gore and says . . . "That's a guy who can tell the truth real easily. . . ." He's had a whole exaggeration problem. He's got maybe fifteen, twenty things that he didn't tell the truth about or you can call it exaggeration.

Sharing views on Al Gore on CNN Capital Campaign *during the presidential campaign, March 2000:*

★ The Clinton-Gore record on campaign finance reform is probably the most disgraceful of any group of candidates in the history of America. So when Al Gore raises campaign finance reform, I think right across the screen you see the word *hypocrisy.* And that's devastating for Al Gore.

On the Clintons:

★ It's the amazing ability that the Clintons have to spin an attack on their opponent when there's a legitimate question about a great ethical lapse on their part.

★ I think we need a big change from the Clinton era. I think it's about time that America got the Clinton era over, and we moved to something different.

President Clinton's last-minute pardons before leaving office in January 2001 met with some controversy. Particularly questionable was that of financier Marc Rich, who was prosecuted by Giuliani in 1983 and declared a fugitive after fleeing the United States.

★ When I first heard about it, my reaction quite honestly was, no, no, it's a mistake. They must be confused with somebody else. No president would pardon a fugitive. No president would pardon someone on the FBI's top number one list of fugitives for a long, long time. No president would ever pardon someone where the charges are still open that he traded with Iran during the hostage crisis. What president would do that?

★ I agree with pardons. I think pardons play a valuable, useful purpose in recognizing that somebody can change their life, which we shouldn't be so cynical as to not recognize. But how can you possibly pardon someone who's a fugitive, who's run away, who's flouted American laws for . . . sixteen, seventeen years?

★ The answer is that here there was an indictment that was outstanding for sixteen, seventeen years. He ran away, and he was pardoned, and it needs to be investigated. We have to find out what are the answers to this totally unexplained pardon. I think it's quite responsible for Congress to do this.

★ It took me about a day to actually absorb the fact that the president of the United States actually pardoned one of our most notorious fugitives.

On President Clinton's controversial pardons:

★ There are a lot of things you can't change; it doesn't mean you don't find out why they happened.

★ This is an important power the president possesses. It should be done honorably.

★ I don't think anybody can say it's unreasonable for the Senate and the House to want to figure out what happened here. If for no other reason than to vindicate in the future the president's awesome power, and important power to pardon. I should emphasize, I agree with pardons. I think pardons are a good thing.

★ I think a pardon is a valuable thing. And President Clinton has put it in real question here.

★ I prosecuted a lot of cases; I also recommended a lot of pardons. I believe that people can straighten themselves out. I believe that people can get in trouble, make a mistake, get over it and it's important for the president to be able to have the ability to pardon them. But until we get the answers to this question, that whole process is put in some jeopardy of being misunderstood by the public.

★ Here's the thing that is very dangerous about what the president is saying. The president has concluded now that they were wrongfully indicted. However, the way he went about it was just to talk to the defense lawyers. This would be a very, very strange thing to happen in the future, I mean, virtually every indictment in America would be dismissed if all you did was talk to the defense lawyers.

★ Maybe there's a good answer here from former president Clinton, maybe there isn't. But it needs to be investigated.

★ The more that the Clinton people discuss this, the more questions they raise about how unusual and strange this whole process is. . . . I worked in the Justice Department for more of my life than I have been mayor of New York City. I've probably recommended or seen two thousand pardon recommendations, passed them along to President Ford and President Reagan. . . . There is no explanation for this pardon. You don't pardon a fugitive.

★ Every time the president talks about this, or his people, it seems like more questions are raised rather than answered.

★ Yes, the president has a lot of power, including this one, and I acknowledge that. I think everyone accepts it. The question is, how wisely has the president exercised that power? Has he exercised it wisely? Arbitrarily? Are there more questions than that? All of that is quite legitimate. After all, you know, President Ford was called before the Congress to discuss the Nixon pardon, even though President Ford had the absolute right to give that pardon. Doesn't mean the president doesn't have to answer questions about the exercise of that power.

★ I don't remember a fugitive being pardoned ever before by any president. There may be one like it, but I've never heard of one.

★ A pardon happens when a person has done their time, paid their dues to society, and allegedly straightened themselves out. This man just ran away.

16

The Making of a Mayor: Giuliani's Early Career

──────────── ★ ────────────

A 1961 scholarship application question asked, "Why do you desire a higher education?" Giuliani replied, "To study law or medicine."

Giuliani graduated from Manhattan College in 1965.

★ I was a crammer in college. I read very fast. This was during the era of President Kennedy's speed reading course, the Evelyn Wood speed reading course.

Reflecting on his career path:

★ I wanted to be a doctor. I wanted to be a journalist. . . . I thought about being an Air Force pilot and I had a lot of different dreams and ambitions, and finally, toward the end of college, decided to go to law school, ended up at NYU Law School. And after a week or two of being in law school, I said to myself, "I found the profession that I like and enjoy and really feel fulfilled with." And I was very lucky; I mean, I found something that . . . sort of fit me.

★ Work defines me.

★ My future—whatever it is going to be—will be a better one if I do a good job.

On his 1970 appointment as assistant U.S. attorney for the Southern District of New York:

★ It was the culmination of all my ambitions and desires.

Giuliani described his aim as U.S. attorney for the Southern District of New York "to make the justice system a reality for the criminal."

On gaining experience as a young U.S. attorney, 1970:

★ I enjoyed trying cases so much. . . . I used to go around asking people for trials because I really enjoyed it.

Rejoicing in one of his proudest courtroom moments, the 1974 trial of Congressman Bertram Podell, who pleaded guilty to conspiracy to defraud the United States government during Giuliani's cross-examination:

★ The cross-examination was something trial lawyers have fantasies about.

In August 1985, while serving as U.S. attorney:

★ I am tired of being asked over and over again, "Which type of crime is more dangerous, violent crime or white-collar crime? Organized crime or public corruption? Drug trafficking or arms trafficking?" All of these areas of crime are dangerous and destructive of our society.

Giuliani defended frequent attacks on his excessive media appearances while serving as U.S. attorney:

★ I do err on the side of being open. You've got to communicate with the public. You can't just sit behind a desk and hope things work out all right.

Looking ahead, in 1986, while serving as U.S. attorney:

★ I don't know what the future holds, but I do know that after this job, I'm going to be involved in public service again because I find it very fulfilling.

From a speech given at a 1987 New York Bar dinner:

★ We have convicted more people at a higher level of power than ever before.

In 1987, while serving as U.S. attorney:

★ Knowing myself, even if I might get discouraged with the idea of public office for a period of time, at some point in the future, after I leave this job, I'm going to want to be back in public life, because I enjoy the sense of accomplishment.

In 1987, on his role as U.S. attorney:

★ God didn't appoint me. President Reagan gave me this job.

★ It is my job to hold people responsible for the crimes they commit.

Giuliani briefly considered a Senate run in 1988 while serving as United States attorney. Dedicated to the investigations he was leading, Giuliani decided to save his Senate pursuit until 2000 (from which he withdrew following his prostate cancer diagnosis).

★ We have so many important investigations of criminal activity now under way that I cannot leave unless I'm sure the right person succeeds me.

★ We don't have a lot of time for transition and I need someone with a working, intimate knowledge of all of the details of each of the cases we have been working on. Too much needs to be done.

On his decision to join the law firm of White & Case,
January 1989:

★ It combines a very, very fine group of lawyers, some of
them at the height of professional achievement, and it has a
very warm atmosphere with people who support each other
and help each other.

On deputy U.S. attorney and longtime aide Dennison
Young, Jr.:

★ My view of a deputy is someone who should essentially
know what I know not only so he can make decisions in my
absence, but so I can bounce ideas off someone.

★ My wife used to say, "Why don't you explain to people,
when they accuse you of being a prosecutor, that the thing that
made you work fifteen, sixteen, seventeen hours a day, not take
a vacation for the last two years, is because you really cared
about people and you really understood that your work is
intended to make people's lives better?" Maybe I guess I
thought people assumed that, knew it. Why else would I do it?
I would not assume that people would think that, well, you did
it just for blind ambition or sheer ego. I thought that they
would know that I'm a really nice guy, a normal person.

Giuliani emerged as a tough prosecutor of Wall Street inside traders.

★ It's one of those areas where a prosecutor can feel some real positive accomplishment, because I think it's an area where you can deter criminality. Unlike investigating and prosecuting violent crime or crimes of passion, these are the kinds of crimes that people commit for a reason—for greed. And if you can make the risk of doing it too great, you're going to stop people from doing it.

★ Now is the time to take our city back from the violent criminals on the streets and the white-collar criminals in their office suites.

★ We've got to bring a whole new ethic on Wall Street. That's what all this is about.

In 1987, Giuliani denied accusations that he rushed the indictments of financiers Robert Freeman, Timothy Tabor, and Richard Wigton, executives who were handcuffed and arrested in their offices in front of stunned colleagues but never brought to trial.

★ Speculation by those seeking anonymity is usually questionable at best.

★ Their lawyers were furious that we cuffed them like common criminals. I told them their clients were examples to others not to commit this kind of crime.

On being asked if he regrets his handling of the 1987 securities fraud cases against Freeman, Tabor, and Wigton:

★ Regret? No. As long as you haven't made a decision for a wrong reason, for something unethical, you can't always be regretting.

On prosecuting the younger insider traders:

★ Prison doesn't fit into the lifestyle these people bargained for.

★ I can understand how a young investment banker has been led astray, but do not ask me to sympathize with him.

Giuliani was devoted to bringing members of the Mafia to justice and would not tolerate those who denied the existence of the Mafia.

★ By using the word *Mafia* correctly, you actually help to end the unfair stereotype. By playing word games and denying reality, you increase the prejudice. The most effective way to beat down the prejudice is to beat them down.

Giuliani remembered his father, himself an Italian American, viewing the Mafia as "bullies, as people who had to band together in order to have the courage to do things."

Giuliani was not shy about his attempts to prosecute the Mafia.

★ We want people to hear that this city is the most aggressive in fighting against organized crime.

★ What we have to do is hit 'em high, hit 'em low, and hit 'em in the middle.

★ We will really destroy the power of the Mafia.

★ It is about time law enforcement got as organized as organized crime.

★ Your target is the entity, not the act.

Giuliani defended his publicity during the Mafia investigations.

★ The only way to deliver a deterrent effectively is to publicize it. I want to send a message.

★ I was very lucky, as U.S. attorney, to be in the right place at the right time. I feel proud of it, and I actually feel proud of something else, the fact that I'm Italian American and that I was able to participate in it in a very public way, I think, helped to reduce the stereotype and the prejudice against Italian Americans about connection to the Mafia.

Giuliani's reputation as a fierce Mafia prosecutor became legendary, as this exchange with a stranger boarding an elevator with Giuliani in 1985 shows.

"You're Rudolph Giuliani. I can't believe it. You're the one in the papers—with the mob. Oh, this is a thrill."

To which Giuliani replied, "Frankly, I'm surprised you're not worried about riding the elevator with me."

On the 1987 prosecution of Sicilian Mafia leader Gaetano Badalamenti in a high-profile case which became known as the "Pizza Connection" after it was learned the defendants were running a heroin trafficking operation through pizzerias:

★ To have him in an American court, prosecuted and convicted, was for me a very fulfilling moment for American justice.

★ The "Pizza Connection" case stands almost on its own. It not only attacked the American Mafia but also the Sicilian Mafia. . . . The former head of the Sicilian Mafia, Gaetano Badalamenti . . . used to sit in the hills of Sicily . . . making billions and billions of dollars by destroying young people in New York City.

★ This case established that the highest members of the Mafia were not bigger and more important than the government, that they could be convicted like anybody else.

In 1987, on comparing two loves, the ongoing prosecution of the Mafia and opera:

★ The best analogy is Wagner's Ring of the Nibelungen. We're now in the beginning of the last opera, *Twilight of the Gods.* But it's a five-hour opera, so we've got a long way to go.

Reaction to several death threats received by Giuliani and his associates while prosecuting Mafia leaders:

★ When they become persistent and serious, then for a period of time I'll get protection for an assistant or I'll do some things a little bit differently, but I don't spend a lot of time worrying about it. The tradition in the United States has been that you don't kill prosecutors and you don't kill agents and you don't kill judges.

★ Sure, they threatened to kill me. . . . I prosecuted the commission of the Mafia. We prosecuted a couple hundred organized crime figures. . . . Some of them got pretty angry about it and put out contracts on you.

On comparing the prosecution of insider traders and the Mafia:

★ Insider trading isn't like organized crime cases, where nobody tells you anything. Here you arrest people and they cooperate. There's no loyalty.

★ The rules apply to mob big shots like "Fat Tony" Salerno, and they apply to big shots at Goldman, Sachs, too.

Reflecting in 1991 on some of his top prosecutions which forged his reputation:

★ I get a lot of credit that I don't deserve and a lot of criticism that I don't deserve. On balance, I'm very proud. I bet you can't find a period of time with a greater impact on crime than this.

Giuliani talked about his prosecutions while serving as U.S. attorney, in Newfield and Barrett's book City for Sale:

★ What has surprised me is that Wall Street has responded in a much more positive way to the revelations of corrupt behavior than the political community has. A few years ago, I thought that politics was democratic, that politicians had to be responsive to the people. But it has been the financial community that has understood that public confidence is important, and they have instituted reforms in response to the cases on insider trading. There are now much stricter disclosure requirements in Wall Street firms; the SEC has been given a 30 percent increase in its budget to do enforcement work; the moral climate on Wall Street has improved; lots of stockbrokers and investment bankers have come up to me to compliment the work our office has done. But I have never had a professional politician say anything like that to me. Very little has changed in politics, despite all the convictions.

17

Timeline of a Mayor:
First Run, 1989

---- ★ ----

Giuliani announced his run for mayor of New York City on May 17, 1989.

★ I make one promise and one promise only: I'll clean up New York. On January 1, 1990, the government of New York City will be independent, it will be nonpartisan and damn well will be honest.

★ New York City needs a change in attitude. This is a pivotal year, the sort of year that doesn't come around often. This year, there's a chance to make a real change.

★ Now is the time to take back our city from the violent criminals on our streets and the white-collar criminals in their office suites, from the drug dealers in abandoned buildings and the crooked politicians who have abandoned their oath of office. It is time to restore the reputation of New York, so that once again our city will be known for its libraries, its universities, its culture, its industry, and its spirit—not as it is known today for crime, crack, and corruption.

Speaking in Sunset Park, Brooklyn, 1989:

★ I've got to get this city to stop thinking in categories, to stop thinking of black and white and Hispanic, and gay and heterosexual, and get us to start thinking about people.

Giuliani thought he would be challenging Mayor Ed Koch until Koch was defeated in the primary by David Dinkins. Giuliani had said of Koch:

★ The mayor is like a loafer, not like an old shoe. He should have the grace to move on.

The first question of the 1989 debate between mayoral candidates Giuliani and David Dinkins focused on a major theme of the race, "How to foster racial harmony," to which Giuliani replied:

★ No one person has a monopoly on that.

Giuliani was not shy in sharing his views of the state of the city.

★ If we keep going merrily along, this city's going down.

He reminded the voters of Dinkins's controversial income tax and financial practices.

★ People usually don't run for mayor of the city of New York who haven't paid their taxes for four years. People don't usually run for mayor of New York who are involved in so many violations of the law and ethical duties.

Giuliani later said of Dinkins:

★ If I had his record, I'd be kind of embarrassed to show my face.

On the campaign trail in 1989:

★ This city is a heavily Democratic town. I think if the Jewish community knew me better, I would get 80 percent of the vote, as we share many values. This is a city in decline, and if you are happy with the last sixteen years then elect another clubhouse Democrat.

On November 7, 1989, Giuliani lost his first bid for mayor to David Dinkins by less than fifty thousand votes, but promised the people of New York that he would be back.

★ And I assure you, I am not going to fade away. I look forward to the future. A future with you, and with New York.

★ I think however an election comes out, there are always things you'd go back and do differently.

Looking ahead, in 1991:

★ It would be a net plus for me if people attack my record as U.S. attorney. If I could be as successful a mayor as I was a U.S. attorney, the city would be out of trouble.

18

Timeline of a Mayor:
First Term

--------------------- ★ ---------------------

Giuliani ran again and was elected 107th mayor of the city of New York on November 2, 1993.

★ People say to me, "Why do you want to be mayor of New York City, you must be crazy." What I say is, "You have to be crazy not to be mayor of New York City."

★ This election is not about race. It is about crime, drugs, schools, jobs, and health care.

On David Dinkins's administration, while both were campaigning for mayor in October 1993:

★ Unfortunately, this administration didn't seize on the opportunities to really try and initiate things in this city. To find innovation, you've got to go somewhere else other than in New York City.

On David Dinkins, during the campaign:

★ The mayor in this city no longer makes decisions. If you hold him responsible, he finds five other people to point the finger at.

★ The reason the morale of the police department of the city of New York is so low is one reason, and one reason alone: David Dinkins.

On the Dinkins administration:

★ I knew this administration would not be competent.

★ This was symbolic government, not substantive government.

After Dinkins ran ads portraying Giuliani as a threat to the city, while both campaigned for mayor in 1993:

★ He knows he can't get your vote based on his record. What he wants to do is to frighten you from voting for me.

Giuliani used Dinkins's handling of the February 1993 school stabbing death of 15-year-old Angel Jimenez by a classmate to illustrate his stance on crime during the campaign.

★ I don't want to ever have to give the answer the mayor gave, which is you can never have enough metal detectors. That isn't an answer. That's an alibi. The answer is, "Dammit, I'm going to find enough money to have enough metal detectors!" That's how to deal with a problem.

From a spring 1993 campaign fund-raiser:

★ We don't ask anyone to sacrifice individual ideologies. We have to get down to work and make this city work fairly for all the boroughs and all ethnic, religious, and racial groups. We have a city to save.

Asked by CNN's Bernard Shaw what he will do about undecided voters for mayor, October 1993:

★ Not go to sleep—and try to meet with every single one of them if I possibly can and convince them that we are the hope, really, for reform and change in New York City.

Giuliani urged that he would be ready to manage the city if he won the election.

★ I think I have a capacity for growth and change. Despite the image, I'm not a rigid person. I'm a different person than I was ten years ago. I've grown, and I hope I continue to do that.

November 1993, Mayor-elect Giuliani addresses his new city.

★ I'm standing before you as the next mayor of New York City. It happened . . . because I asked you to believe in me, and you did. And I'm very grateful to you. You gave me your vote and I accept the responsibility that goes with it. You have my pledge that I will work to fulfill your expectations, and hopefully even exceed them. From the very start, and tonight is that start, I want New York to know and understand my stated goal. My administration will be universal in its concern, sensitive to our diversity, and evenhanded in every way possible. Nobody—no ethnic, religious, or racial group—will escape my care, my concern, and my attention.

★ Give me the opportunity to show you that I can serve the entire city equally and fairly and with dedication. And give me the opportunity to do that, not just with words, but with deeds. If you do, then I believe that we can all come together as New Yorkers, as we should.

On his new administration:

★ By and large, there'll be a house cleaning, but there'll be some exceptions.

★ People voted for change in New York City government. I believe that's what I have to give them.

Looking ahead at his role as mayor, December 1993:

★ New Yorkers will throw you out if you don't produce, as they should. New York is a very tough city, but a very caring and compassionate one and people of New York City are very intelligent and you have got to produce.

★ As far as I'm concerned, at this point, it doesn't matter who people voted for. Voted for me, against me, whatever. I have to serve all the people of New York City and they have to all be represented in the government of New York City.

From the mayor's 1994 Inauguration Speech:

★ On the second day of January of 1994, I dedicate my administration to you, the people of New York City. May God bless each one of us as we prepare to give our children a stronger, healthier city. It should be so and it will be so.

★ As of this moment the expressions of cynicism—New York is not governable, New York is not manageable, New York is not worth it—all of these I declare politically incorrect.

★ The era of fear has had a long enough reign.

★ I ask of you what I demand of myself—greet tomorrow with a determined capacity to overcome any problem. Dream, believe, plan, and work with me.

★ On this day of new beginning, I give you my solemn pledge to summon our courage, to raise our hopes, and to build our confidence.

Giuliani's seven-year-old son, Andrew, became a household name after accompanying his father to the podium for the swearing in and playing to the cameras during the formal proceeding. Giuliani observed:

★ I'm going to have a co-addressee, I guess, Andrew.

★ He took the oath, he participated in the inaugural speech. This may mean that I now share power with him. So we're going to try to work out with Andrew a delegation of his power back to me.

★ We're trying to figure out what's the legal effect of what he did yesterday. Paul Crotty [the city's corporation counsel] is concerned that not only did he take the oath, he gave an inaugural address.

At the start of his term as mayor, 1994:

★ The opportunity to rebuild New York is right here, it's right now, it's been handed to us and what we have to do is seize it.

Looking ahead to city reform, July 1994:

★ I believe that you create a better society by setting higher standards and expecting better behavior from people.

*Giuliani described South African president Nelson
Mandela's 1994 visit to Gracie Mansion as "one of the
great moments that I'll always remember as mayor of New
York City. He came to Gracie Mansion, visited, and I think
probably one of the things I'll remember best about it is
how he treated my children . . . they just . . . immediately
ran up to him, he spent a lot of time with them."*

On New York City and New York State, November 1994:

★ It's impossible for the state of New York to be successful if New York City isn't because we contribute so much to the economy of the state.

★ The fact is, that I view people as people, and I don't subscribe to some of the so-called politically correct notions . . . I believe you should treat all people the same way. And that's the way in which you can create a society in which everybody kind of moves forward and you don't continue this friction into a second generation and a third and a fourth.

From a March 1995 National Press Club address:

★ The central problem with New York City is not realizing that New York City is not a city of problems, that New York City is a city of assets that far outweigh every single one of those problems. We're a city that produces more wealth than any city in America. We're a city that is the world capital for so many different endeavors, whether it's finance, communications, entertainment, and understanding that we can use those assets to help address each and every one of those problems.

From the mayor's 1995 State of the City Address:

★ If the past year has proved anything, it is that the answers to our problems will come from us—New Yorkers. We are the experts on urban life . . . on its problems . . . and its promise.

★ We must make the rest of the nation understand that when we ask for programs for New York City, we are merely seeking a return on the investment we are making in the rest of America.

From the mayor's 1995 testimony before the Subcommittee on Government Reform and Oversight:

★ When I came into office, I was determined to change the direction of New York City, and set it on a course for growth, prosperity, and hope.

★ We have altered the direction of New York City and changed its fundamental course. And if it can be done in New York City, it can be done anywhere.

★ Nothing is more fundamental to the philosophy of my administration than the goal of improving the quality of life for each citizen . . . every day . . . in all parts of New York City.

★ Making our city a safer and more decent place to live is in the best interest of everyone.

*Giuliani raved about his communications department in
April 1995.*

★ I think they have done a remarkable job in conveying the
message of an administration that whether you've noticed it or
not, has made more change in this city in sixteen months than
I think has ever been the case before, with the possible excep-
tion of the first sixteen months of Fiorello LaGuardia. The
people of the city know that, and I know that because I talk to
the people of the city probably more often than any other
mayor.

*From the mayor's 1996 address to the Young
Men's/Women's Real Estate Association of New York:*

★ I am pleased to report that New York City is back. There is
a sense of optimism in the neighborhoods of New York City
that we haven't seen in some time. Whether it's Times Square,
or Wall Street, or Fordham Road, or Myrtle Avenue, or
Flushing Avenue, or Bay Street, wherever you go in New York
City. . . .

The mayor addressed the community of Montoursville, Pennsylvania, after the July 1996 crash of TWA Flight 800 en route to Paris. Sixteen students and five chaperones traveling to France on a French Club trip were killed in the crash.

★ In New York City, we are so big that we sometimes think that our strength comes from our skyscrapers and the tremendous amount of income they produce, or we think that our strength comes from our museums or our theaters, and the music and the arts and the culture that they provide. And very often in America we think our strength comes from our military, or our farms, or our industry, or even from our natural resources. These things all provide strength, but Montoursville, you reminded us, all of us, even in New York City, that our true strength, that our real foundation derives from something much more basic. It comes from our families, from our homes, from our churches, our synagogues, our communities. It comes from people relying on each other and being able to count on their support . . . you also showed us there is something even more important than justice, you've showed all the world that even in times of grief, too great to bear, too massive to even contemplate, the love of a family, the love of a friend, the love of a neighbor, transcends the greatest of sorrows . . . it's okay to need help and it's all right to cry, it's necessary to share pain.

Giuiliani said of the tragedy:

★ I can't remember a twenty-four-hour period worse than this one since I've been the mayor.

Honoring those who aided in the rescue effort of the 1996 crash of TWA Flight 800:

★ Together, we showed that the very worst of times can bring out the very best of humanity, as New Yorkers, Americans, and the nations of the world rallied to share their strength.

From the mayor's 1996 State of the City Address:

★ New York City once again is a success story . . . in fact . . . it is many success stories. In many areas, we are a model for the rest of the nation. We are the American benchmark for excellence.

From the mayor's 1996 Address on Tolerance:

★ We must create a better understanding both of government's power and its limitations . . . and at the same time foster a deeper appreciation for the responsibilities and capabilities of the individual. Instead of a war on drugs, we must talk about strategies for reducing drugs. Instead of a war on poverty, we must talk about programs to alleviate its worst effects and to move people into lives of independence and self-sufficiency. Instead of looking for the government program that will eliminate racism, government must try to educate, spreading a message of tolerance, equality, and inclusion. And with each of these concerns—drugs, poverty, racism—we must recognize that the real solution won't come from a government office . . . but from within ourselves. If the past thirty years has taught us anything, it is that the solutions to our greatest problems will come from the smallest units within society—individuals.

From the mayor's Year-End Briefing, December 1996:

★ The city of New York needed to show vast substantive improvement and we have and ultimately I think I would prefer to be a mayor that has accomplished historic things for the city that haven't been accomplished before, that has made people's lives safer, that have helped children more, that have set the city on a solid course of real progress than just pandering to people and telling them the things they want to hear and be personally popular, but have their programs and their substantive approach to government rejected.

Thoughts on his first term:

★ I am proud of the fact that in our first year we have undertaken no less than the redefinition and reinvention of New York City's government. I am proud of all that we've accomplished, and I'm aware of how far we have to go. . . .

★ Over the past three and half years, we've dispelled the defeatism that had once prevailed in our city. We are now a city that welcomes growth and opportunity and our many successes have become a model for the world. No longer are we a city that is afraid to rethink the status quo and come up with a better way. We are constantly striving and succeeding in making many of our city agencies more accountable, efficient, and effective.

★ In New York City, we've seen how effective management can yield successful results. Throughout the country and throughout the world New York City has become known as a place that welcomes growth and progress, but even more importantly, new ideas.

★ When I first came into office three and half years ago, there was the feeling on the part of many that New York City was headed toward an inevitable state of decline. . . . Times have changed. Today we've reinvented government, our city, and our way of life. We've become a city where new ideas are welcomed and actually put to the test. Some of these ideas work better than others, but we are continually thinking and looking for solutions. And that's what matters.

★ It's my sincere hope that the federal government can learn from the unparalleled success we enjoy in New York.

★ I think the reason the city is doing so well, the reason the city is doing so much better with jobs, the reason its economy is doing better, the reason its budget is doing better, isn't me alone, it's the people that I've been able to establish a real teamwork with. I'm very, very fortunate to have enormously talented people that are working for the city of New York, which is the reason why the city's cleaner, the city is much safer than it's been before.

★ I am interested in this job. I am running for reelection for it. I enjoy it very much. It's really a fulfilling job and I have a rule that I follow which I follow through all the other jobs that I have. I do the one that I have been elected to, appointed to, or been hired for, and I don't start thinking about the future. Let the future take care of itself.

19

Timeline of a Mayor: Second Term

─────────── ★ ───────────

On November 4, 1997, Giuliani was the first Republican mayor in New York City to get elected to a second term since Fiorello LaGuardia in 1941.

★ If I do a good job, I have a future. If I don't do a very good job as mayor of New York City, I don't have a future.

Asked in November 1997, following his reelection, if he saw the presidency in his future:

★ I don't see anything in my future right now but taking the oath of office on January 1.

From his Victory Speech, 1997:

★ We made the world realize that change is possible. So today, New York is a better place to live than it was four years ago. Today, our quality of life is improved and we're much more united as one city, one standard. And most New Yorkers believe, as I do, that our best days are yet to come.

★ We have to do a better job to include all of you. We have to reach out to all of you. If we haven't, I apologize. I'm sorry. It's my personal commitment we will try endlessly and tirelessly.

★ We must continue to move forward instead of turning back the clock to the policies of the past.

★ I am dedicated to fulfilling New York's historic and most important role as America's most caring, most compassionate, and most generous city.

At the start of his second term, in 1998:

★ If you think that I've run out of enthusiasm for the job because I am a lame duck, watch out!

★ When you look at the number of possibilities that we have in the city, if we work together for the benefit of the entire city, there's nothing that we really can't accomplish.

From the mayor's Second Inaugural Speech, "The Agenda for Permanent Change," January 1998:

★ Four years ago, when I stood here and said "New York City is the capital of the world," there was doubt. There was fear. There was the feeling that New York City's best days were behind us. I didn't accept that. Many of you didn't accept it either. And over the last few years, in an exercise of human will and determination, you and I together have changed the direction of the city more than in any four-year period in history.

All that we have done, all that we must continue to do together, is based on continuing to liberate the human spirit, understanding that liberty is a balance of freedom and responsibility, of rights and obligations.

★ Let history say of us that we used our great wealth and strength to support the creation of beauty and that, more than any time before us, we made the opportunity to experience beauty enter the lives of all New Yorkers to lift them to a greater understanding of the uniqueness of their humanity.

★ I think the general feeling among people around the country and in New York was New York had seen its best days—used to be a great city, still is going to be a significant city, but it's seen its best day. I didn't accept that.

Speaking at the 1998 Annual Young Leadership
Conference:

★ Just five years ago, New York City was riddled by pes-
simism and cynicism. Too many people were overcome by
these feelings and overwhelmed by our obstacles rather than
invigorated by the challenges ahead . . . rather than being filled
with hope for the possibility of constructive, progressive
change. For a majority of people both inside and outside the
city, New York City was out of control. As a city, we had
become known for our problems, not for our strengths. If you
asked people around the country what they thought of New
York, they most likely would have said we were a city that was
dangerous, out of control—an unmanageable city. But over
the last five years, fueled by the leadership of so many people
cooperating to make the city a better place, we've changed the
spirit of New York City. Because we refused to give in to pes-
simism or cynicism, both the reality and perception of the city
have changed.

On his decision to boycott the 1998 Grammy Awards after
Grammy chief Michael Green allegedly verbally harassed a
mayoral aid:

★ If you abuse a person who works for the city of New York
and take advantage of them and yell curses at them and swear
at them and tell them that you're going to kill them, then I
don't want to do business with you.

Praising New York City's record job growth in 1998:

★ These job numbers again confirm the fact that New York is the city people throughout the world turn to for leadership as the capital of the world.

On surviving Hurricane Floyd, September 1999:

★ The tougher the problem, the more New Yorkers respond. It's unbelievable.

Concluding a speech on the merits of City Charter reform, October 1999:

★ We've come a long way as a city since the early 1990s. Let's make sure we never go back.

Giuliani claimed that the controversial 1999 Brooklyn Museum of Art exhibit Sensation *was a sacrilegious depiction of the Virgin Mary. His attempt to cut the museum's funding was denied by a judge, citing First Amendment rights. Giuliani's response:*

★ Nobody is trying to suppress this exhibit. I'm very much opposed to it. But what I'm saying is hard-earned public tax dollars should not be used for what I consider to be—and I think many people in the city—a desecration of religion. . . .

★ I don't think it's appropriate for taxpayer dollars to be used to aggressively desecrate religion, whether it's my own religion, the Catholic religion, the Jewish religion, the Protestant religion, the Muslim religion.

★ This is not an issue of suppression. These people have a right to do it. They just can't do it on the hard-earned dollars of the taxpayer.

★ I think this show is disgusting. It is a disgusting show. I think that it's a terrible, terrible use of government funds.

★ I generally have a definition of art, which is if I can do it, it's not art. And in this particular case, anybody could do it.

★ Taxpayer dollars shouldn't be on either side of this dispute. We can't support religion. We shouldn't support vicious attacks on religion, either.

In disagreement with Hillary Rodham Clinton on Sensation:

★ She agrees with using public funds to attack and bash the Catholic religion.

Maintaining his stance on the Brooklyn Museum of Art exhibit Sensation, *on* Meet the Press, *1999:*

★ Maybe it would be easier for you and others to understand if this were another racial, religious, or ethnic group, but 30 percent of the people that are highly offended about their religion, their national symbols, their sensibilities being attacked is a very large percentage of people that the mayor has a right to defend. And what I'm saying is very simple: Nobody wants to suppress it. Put it in a private museum. Pay for it yourself. Do not take money out of the pockets of that 30 percent of the people where you're doing tremendous damage to their sensibilities, their views, their ideas. In America . . . what it means is we have to all respect each other. And that 30 percent is also entitled to respect.

As the former third-ranking official in the Justice Department and director of the United States Immigration and Naturalization Service, Giuliani felt strongly about the April 2000 case of Elián Gonzales, the child who survived after a boat containing Cuban refugees, including his mother, sank off the Florida coast. The INS denied a petition for his asylum in the United States and he returned to Cuba to live with his father.

★ I think the boy should be given permanent resident status in the United States, or even citizenship, so that his case can be resolved in the family court, not by the Immigration and Naturalization Service. They are not experts on children. They have no knowledge of what's in the best interest of the child. I say this most respectfully. They don't care what's in the best interest of the child. What they care about is international politics when they're acting at their best. The child is irrelevant.

★ These decisions are being made in the White House, they're being made for political reasons, and they're being made for diplomatic reasons. All well and good. But what about the little boy?

★ And left out of all of this is his mother. His mother died in order to give him the blessings of freedom, democracy, the rule of law.

In May 2000, following the shooting of Patrick Dorismond, killed during a confrontation with undercover police, Giuliani was criticized for publicly releasing his juvenile record.

★ I made a mistake. I should have also conveyed the human feeling that I had, the compassion, the loss of the mother. I think if I could do it over again, I would have tried to balance it more.

★ The reality is that over the long term, people will see that it was the correct response.

In August 2000, opposing PETA's (People for the Ethical Treatment of Animals) controversial billboard campaign featuring Mayor Giuliani, without his permission, and suggesting a connection between dairy products and cancer:

★ I think it's highly objectionable and I also think it gives an incorrect message. . . . There is no connection between my prostate cancer, or anyone else's, and drinking milk.

★ I also think that they are violating the civil rights law in New York, which says that you can't use someone for commercial purposes without getting their permission.

★ They give the impression that there's a connection between drinking milk and prostate cancer, which is not true and largely disputed. And they frighten people about a product that is a good product. Why are they doing it? They're not doing it because they care about cancer; this is not the American Cancer Association. They are worried about the cows; their motive for this is worrying about cows, not worrying about human beings.

Promoting the expansion of the New York Public Library, January 2001:

★ Don't you love the smell of a good book?

In February 2001, again outraged at the Brooklyn Museum of Art exhibit Yo Mama's Last Supper, *a photograph depicting Jesus Christ as a nude black woman, Giuliani said:*

★ I think that what they did is disgusting. It's outrageous. If it were done against another group there'd be an outcry in the city.

★ If we had decency standards, I submit that this photograph would never be exhibited in a building funded by the taxpayers.

On the July 2001 final budget agreement of the mayor and the City Council:

★ In this final budget we have once again demonstrated that a city in control of its destiny is committed to fiscal responsibility and tax policies that reward the entrepreneurial spirit that has always made New York City the capital of the world.

Reaction to a lawsuit filed by Eliot Spitzer, the state's attorney general, to maintain gardens on potential public housing property sites:

★ Gardens are nice, but affordable housing doesn't grow on trees.

Hailing the November 2001 return of the Concorde, the world's fastest passenger jet, following the July 2000 crash that killed over one hundred people:

★ This is a wonderful thing for the city. The friendship between New York and London and between New York and Paris is very strong, and over the last eight weeks it has become even stronger.

During Michael Bloomberg's run for mayor:

★ In New York we only elect Republicans when we're in real trouble. So, in a way, my administration had not created the mood to help Republicans win.

★ I told him the only advantage to being a Republican in New York City is the Democratic primary, where they kill each other.

*Following the November 2001 election of Michael
Bloomberg as mayor of New York City:*

★ Starting tomorrow, it's going to be my job to try to help
the new mayor to get ready for a very difficult job.

*Following the November 2001 crash of Flight 587 in
Rockaway, Queens, just weeks after the World Trade Center
attacks, President George W. Bush remarked to Giuliani
that New York is being tested again. Giuliani replied, "Mr.
President, we'll pass the test like we did last time."*

Thoughts on his second term:

★ The greatest satisfaction that I have now is when I talk to
people and they tell me how New York has changed and they
say to me, "New York is much better than it was five or six
years ago," and "This is the best city in the world."

★ Thanks to New Yorkers with courage, vision, and imagina-
tion, our city has become one of the world's cleanest, safest,
and exciting places to visit—reaffirming the fact that New
York City truly is the capital of the world.

★ The thing I think that I take the most pride in is the spirit
of the city has come back. The city has a great spirit.

★ New York City was considered a metropolis that could not
be governed. But this administration proved otherwise, making great strides forward in several key areas.

★ I believe most people think—and I believe, and some people don't agree with this—that I've had great success as the mayor of New York City in many, many ways, in ways there hadn't been success before, making the city the safest large city in America, producing more jobs than we ever had in a three-year period of time, new jobs, reviving the economy, tourism, welfare down . . . a change in spirit. The city is a place that now appears to be having a great future as opposed to where it was seven or eight years ago. But there are people in the city that feel that they haven't been reached by that. There are people that feel that I don't care about them. There are people that feel that I don't take them into equal consideration. And I always tried to deal with that with objective facts, I always tried to deal with that by showing, "Well, you know, how can you say that? I've done as much for you as I have for anyone else. I've done more in some cases. Look how these neighborhoods have been revived, look how crime has gone down, look how many more jobs there are now, look how many more people are working." So . . . maybe there's a different form of communication that I have to learn. Maybe it comes out of that—that I want people to respect me more than love me, and I have to figure out how to do that, how to make . . . in good conscience and honest to what I believe, I have to make people get to see the real me, what I'm trying to do, what I'm trying to accomplish, and break down some of the barriers that I've created. Maybe it came from my personality.

20

The 2000 Senate Race

★

Talking to David Letterman about his July 1999 political fund-raiser in Little Rock, Arkansas, former residence of Hillary Rodham Clinton:

★ I'm gonna get off the airplane in Little Rock, and I'm gonna say [with Southern accent], "I've never lived here, I've never worked here, I ain't never been here, but I think it'd be cool to be your senator."

On Hillary Rodham Clinton and Giuliani's beloved New York Yankees:

★ I don't remember seeing her at a Yankee game during the hundreds of times that I was there, and so I'm willing to accept anybody at their word and if she became a Yankee fan in Chicago, okay, she became a Yankee fan in Chicago. . . .

Giuliani cut short his bid for the United States Senate following his cancer diagnosis in May 2000. Before deciding to withdraw, the race had pitted Giuliani against First Lady Hillary Rodham Clinton, the first wife of a sitting president to run for public office. Clinton, who drew some criticism for running for senator of a state in which she had never resided, went on to win the election.

★ I think that the arguments and the claim that I have of being the senator from my native state that I have served for many, many years as the mayor of New York City and as United States attorney is a pretty darn strong claim, so I am more than willing to put that . . . to the test.

★ I am from New York. I was born here. I was born in Brooklyn. I've been the United States attorney, the mayor of New York City, and I have a record of success on issues that are very, very important. So, you know, from my point of view, I think this campaign is about ideas, and it should be about your record, where you've had a chance to put your ideas into practice.

★ I like the idea of having held public office first before you can run for president, to prove yourself, or hold public office first before you run for senator so you can prove yourself. I also prefer the idea that you run for the Senate in the state that you come from.

On the possibility of Hillary Clinton's run:

★ If Hillary ran, I would challenge her to a debate on baseball, New York baseball. Who knows more about the Yankees and the Mets?

On Hillary Rodham Clinton's run for New York senator:

★ One of the debates that we're going to have is, we're both going to have to get in our car at LaGuardia Airport, and get home by ourselves. And we're going to have to figure out who can find their way. In fact, maybe I can show her the way to Chappaqua.

★ I have a real connection to this place. This is a real, authentic candidacy for the Senate, not something . . . strictly by someone who moved in a couple of days ago, virtually, and is kind of like reading what political analysts tell her to say.

★ It's a little like Newton's law, right? For every action, there's an equal and opposite reaction. And the equal and opposite reaction is on the Republican side.

Asked by Larry King in February 2000 what he thinks of a Senate race against Hillary Clinton:

★ It'll be terrific. It's two very different philosophies.

In March 2000, Giuliani once again led New York City's annual St. Patrick's Day Parade while his campaign rival, Hillary Clinton, walked a few blocks behind.

★ This is her first parade. This is my twentieth.

Reaction to an early 2000 poll showing Giuliani behind Hillary Clinton for the first time:

★ I don't use polls to guide my activity as mayor.

Giuliani announced he had been diagnosed with cancer on April 27, 2000, creating speculation that he may withdraw his bid for senator.

★ In fairness to me, to the Senate race, to the Republican Party, to all the parties and everybody else, you need some time to think about it, and I really need to know what the course of treatment is going to be before I can evaluate it. So the answer is, I guess, the same answer about the Senate race that I would have about the course of treatment. I don't know the answer to that yet. I hope that I'd be able to run, but the choice that I'm going to make about treatment is going to be contingent upon the treatment that gives me the best opportunity to have a full and complete cure. And then after I determine that, then I will figure out, does it make sense to run this year or doesn't it, or whatever?

★ You know, sometimes I think yes and sometimes I think no. And it isn't right to take on that commitment if you don't feel a strong sense of certitude that you can complete it.

In May 2000, joking with reporters who questioned whether he would remain in the Senate race:

★ Rumors of my demise are greatly exaggerated.

On May 19, 2000, Giuliani announced that he had decided to withdraw from the Senate race following his cancer diagnosis.

★ This is not the right time for me to run for office. If it were six months ago or if it were a year from now or the timing were a little different, maybe it would be different, but it isn't different and that's the way life is.

★ I've decided that what I should do is to put my health first.

★ I believe this is the right decision. And I think somehow, somewhere, some way this is all for the best.

★ It doesn't mean there's going to be a new Rudy; I think that's silly. I think maybe it's going to be . . . somebody who grows from the fact that you confront your limits, you confront your mortality. You realize you're not a superman and you're just a human being.

★ Politics is not as important in my life as I once thought it was.

★ I wanted to run. It was very, very hard to decide not to run. And the fact is that . . . I had no idea that I was going to have cancer. I mean, that's not something that I planned on. . . . I wanted the job. I felt that I could carry on many of the things that I had done as mayor of New York City in that job and spread it to the whole state. And I feel that a lot of what I've accomplished in the job, the good things that I've accomplished in the job, come out of a fairly consistent philosophy of how government inter-reacts with people, which could easily apply itself to the state, to the nation. So I was looking forward to it, and I'd prepared myself for it. And I was ready to do it and wanted to do it.

★ I'm not thinking right now about politics, honestly. . . . I can't say it's the furthest thing from my thoughts. It'll never be. I love politics. . . . There's a whole aspect of politics that I love. But right now, I've moved it down the priority list and . . . and the thing that I felt good about as I made the decision, and this morning, I finally figured out that politics is not my life. My life is about things that are closer to you and deeper than that. . . . Maybe then if I engage in politics later or practice law again or do other things, I'll do it even better.

★ And I thank God that it gives me another . . . eighteen months to be the mayor of New York City, which I love very, very much. It's really my deep passion, the love for the people of this city and the love of this city. And I'm going to devote the time that I've been given, the extra time that I've been given, not only to do the things that we have done and things that we've accomplished together and the remarkable things that have been done, or to overcome maybe some of the barriers that maybe I placed there, and figure out how to overcome them. I don't know the answer to that yet. I don't know exactly how you do that. But I'm going to try very hard to do that.

On being asked by NBC News's Tim Russert if he regrets his decision to withdraw from the United States Senate Race, May 2000:

★ No, I don't think you can have regrets. . . . It was the most difficult decision in my life. I think I still have to make the more difficult decision about treatment. But, no, I thought about it for a long time, agonized over it, stayed up late at night, talked to every one of my close friends about it. Decided at different ways, without exaggeration, maybe fifty times, thought I would do it, would not do it, couldn't do it, can't do it, different ways of doing it, staying at home. And what I found was that it was severely interfering with my being able to confront cancer and figure out what to do about it and to just give myself the maximum chance of whatever treatment I decide to recover and that my priorities were not right, that my priorities should have been from the beginning my health, the people that I love, caring for them, having them care for me, my job as mayor, which I also love in a very passionate way.

PART IV

GIULIANI ON THE ISSUES

——————— ★ ———————

21

Crime

————————— ★ —————————

Giuliani was committed to fighting all levels of crime and making the streets of New York City safer. Crime dropped 64 percent during his terms.

★ When you reduce crime, you restore people's freedom.

★ When people feel that they can walk down their street at any hour without being threatened, then the civic life of neighborhoods begins to thrive. Businesses will only invest their capital—and families will only invest their future— where they feel safe.

At a 1996 New York City Police Department promotion ceremony:

★ New York City is making true progress in the fight against crime. We are doing what they said could not be done—we are bringing about dramatic reductions in crime.

Praising crime reduction efforts in New York City:

★ People throughout the world no longer see New York City as a national symbol of the plague of crime and violence. Now people see New York as a safe, decent place, and as a leader in fighting crime.

★ If you improve the quality of life in a community, crime goes down.

On his attempts to stop crime at the most basic level— broken windows, intimidating squeegee men, and destructive graffiti:

★ We can't be too busy to pay attention to those things because those are the things that underlie the problems of crime.

★ We have instituted in New York City what we call the broken windows theory. What that means is we take small things seriously, instead of what we used to do, which is to ignore small things. . . . The broken windows theory is Professor Wilson's theory of about twenty years ago that says you got to fix the first broken window, otherwise the whole house can fall down.

Speaking in 1998 on the decrease in graffiti in NYC:

★ The real difference is the feeling that you get when you walk around the city. It's a feeling of shared respect and peace—not disorder and contempt for public and private property.

On eliminating all levels of crime:

★ You can ignore the problem and say, "Gee, I'm such a big, fuzzy-headed liberal that I'm going to walk away from it." That's New York in the 1980s. That's New York City with two thousand murders.

★ No one thing is going to solve the problem of crime. You really can't even solve the problem of crime. You can reduce it more effectively. That's what we should be talking about.

★ I know we're never going to be absolutely crime-free. And we're probably never going to be absolutely drug-free. But I believe that if you aim for moral and decent ideals and even if you fall short of that ideal, you're going to vastly improve society. But instead, if we define our values down, and keep saying we can't do anything about drugs, we can't do anything about welfare, we can't do anything about crime, we can't do anything about dirt on our streets, we can't do anything about deterioration, then not only does the problem become the main worry, it inevitably gets much worse.

On gun control:

★ We have a horrendous number of guns in this country.

★ I do believe . . . it isn't the fundamental cause of crime. . . . Guns make the problem that we have worse. They don't create the problem that we have.

August 1994, endorsing President Clinton's crime bill:

★ This is what I believe in! This bill is as much my bill as it is anyone else's. I've worked on this bill.

★ And if we've become so partisan that a mayor can't stand up with the president when he agrees with the president, then we've really let Washington kind of drive us all crazy.

★ And there are times in which even Republicans and Democrats can find a way to agree.

★ Anything that gets handguns and automatic weapons out of our streets, out of our cities, out of our states, I'm in favor of.

★ Things are changing, and the automatic weapon, the machine gun, is much more available than people realize. There's no point in not banning them. I don't understand why we can't ban them.

★ We put more controls on the driving of an automobile than we do on the possession of attack weapons and that is irrational.

22

Drugs

★

★ Drug abuse enslaves the mind and destroys the soul, causing people to abandon their duties, their children, their friends, their jobs, their education—everything that is worthwhile in life, everything that makes a city great.

★ Drug use is one of the nation's most difficult and complex problems, but I refuse to accept the notion that somehow it is beyond our reach and we must resign ourselves to it.

★ Drugs rob you of a free will and a free life.

★ We should have a drug-free New York, and we should have a drug-free America. There is no reason why we shouldn't aim for the ideal goal of a society in which, if not every single individual, the maximum number of people possible can live their lives free of drugs. If you aim for that goal, you'll get closer to it.

★ We get to a drug-free America by arresting the people who are selling drugs, putting them in jail for a very, very long time, and recognizing the fact that people who sell those dangerous drugs are very much like murderers because they take people's lives from them. . . .

On Defense Attorney Judd Burstein's proposal to make heroin available to addicts, October 1982:

★ Murder is a reality also, but we don't permit it. Rape is a reality and we don't permit it. Permitting people to shoot poison in their veins is a terribly inhumane way to deal even with them, and to try to paint that in a humane way I think is a monstrous misrepresentation to the American people. And I don't think . . . this country is ready for it, and I'd be very sad if we ever reached a day when we were ready for decriminalizing heroin.

On the 1983 inauguration of his Narcotics Task Force while at the Department of Justice:

★ I can't think of anything we could do that would be more positive for the twelve largest cities than to cut down the heroin traffic by a substantial amount. The quality of life is going to change, and it's *attainable;* it's not impossible.

Speaking on drug eradication at Forest Hills Senior Center in Queens in 1993:

★ The heavy emphasis has got to be on arresting the drug sellers. That doesn't mean completely ignore people who use drugs or who buy the drugs. But the heavy emphasis has to be on the people who sell the drugs, the high-level ones, the middle-level ones, the low-level ones. All of them have to be subjected to the possibility of arrest.

From a 1999 speech, on the lack of drug rehabilitation centers:

★ We're spending money at the worst possible time, when someone has been arrested, rather than the best possible time, when they are seeking treatment.

23

Welfare Reform

★

★ When people have jobs, our city has hope.

★ Work gives people self-worth; dependency robs them of it.

★ In my view, the way I was brought up, it is much more compassionate to lead somebody towards self-sufficiency and work than it is to have a million people depending on welfare.

★ The kindest, the most generous, and most loving way to take care of someone is to respect their independence and give them the ability to take care of themselves.

★ Welfare is many, many things, and many different things to different people. But the thing it is not in the life of a human being or a society is progressive. When you are moving people from work to welfare, when you're moving people from being able to take care of themselves to being dependent on someone else to take care of them, a society is not moving in a progressive direction. It's moving in an opposite direction.

★ A society that's moving in a progressive direction is a society in which there are increasing numbers of people able to take care of themselves, and consequently able to take care of their families, or maybe able to take care of increasing numbers of people: their families, their parents, their in-laws, their neighbors, and others. That's a society that's moving in a healthy direction.

★ The purpose of welfare is to help people temporarily. The best result for welfare is to have someone working as quickly as possible.

On promoting welfare reform in 1998:

★ I think the turnaround that's taking place in the Human Resources Administration (HRA) is remarkable, and wonderful, and it's one of the most beautiful things happening in the city, and I think the turnaround that's taking place in the neighborhoods of New York City is absolutely terrific, and if in fact the work ethic made America great, which it did, the more and more people we can have acquire a true understanding of that work ethic, it's just absolutely impossible to really dream what will actually happen as a result of that.

★ When you release human beings to be free in a responsible way, then human beings create things that nobody ever anticipated.

★ As people acquire this sense and ability of taking care of themselves, they become much more diligent, much better, and much more creative in taking care of the people they love as well.

★ Any form of work that is honest and decent is meaningful work. And this notion that cleaning streets is not meaningful work is terribly insulting to the human spirit. If you can work and take care of your family and not have somebody else take care of you then you are moving in a very positive direction. And any work that is decent and honest gives you the chance to expand, to grow, to grow within yourself, and we want New York City to exude that all throughout the city and permanently into the next century.

★ When students read history books twenty and thirty years from now, they're going to say I took a city of dependency and made it into a city of workers!

★ And if we really mean that we want people to be free and independent, then we want people to have jobs. Because a job is better than any social program invented by the state government or local government.

★ A society in which an increasing number of people have the freedom and independence to make choices for themselves is a society that is progressive, it is a society that has a spirit of optimism, and it is a society that can accomplish a great deal.

★ At the core of our approach to welfare reform is the basic concept of a social contract—that for every right there is a duty, for every benefit an obligation.

From the mayor's 1996 State of the City Address:

★ I will not rest until we've restored all of the jobs we lost in the early nineties and provide all New Yorkers with the opportunity to take care of themselves and their families.

On promoting the city's workfare program in the 1996 State of the City Address:

★ It's about giving someone the ability to handle their own destiny . . . to handle their own life . . . take care of their own family . . . giving them the opportunity to develop the self-worth that comes from having a job, and being able to take care of yourself. . . .

★ I think work is better than welfare and dependency.

★ I believe that a job is by far the best social program.

★ Retaining and creating jobs is one of the highest priorities of my administration.

24

Children

─────────────── ★ ───────────────

In praise of the work of Administration for Children's Services (ACS):

★ Any good parent can tell you that raising a child is the most important and challenging job there is. The amount of love, care, and commitment it requires is enormous. But any mother or father will also tell you that the gifts they get in return for being a parent are immeasurable. Even the most common moments of everyday life—walks to school, quiet time reading together, and talkative meals at the kitchen table—become something special when they are shared with a child.

★ There's nothing more important to a child than a loving family. That's the greatest single gift that we can give a child, because in addition to providing them with that critical support throughout childhood, a stable and permanent home gives a child a much better opportunity to succeed in life.

★ Our children's future is largely shaped by the values of their parents.

★ One of the most important responsibilities of government is to protect children from harm.

★ We must give the hopeless hope, particularly the children.

★ Every child needs and deserves a stable and loving family life.

★ Every family deserves to raise their children in an environment that is safe, one that is free from fear and intimidation.

★ Adoptive parents are parents in the truest sense of the word—people who do not simply give birth to a child, but raise, support, and love a child.

25

Education

───────────── ★ ─────────────

★ Children live what they learn.

★ One of the things I enjoy most about being mayor is visiting schoolchildren, reading with them, and hearing about what they want to be when they grow up.

★ You've got to give young people who have no hope, you have to try to give them hope. When we give up on that, we're really giving up on America.

★ Teaching a child to read is giving that child the key to a future of hope and fulfillment.

★ To remain vibrant and dynamic New York City must be constantly energized and renewed by generations of young people, raised in our neighborhoods, educated in our schools, committed to their city and its continued vitality.

★ The fact is, children respond to standards . . . they rise to the level of their teachers' expectations. They need to be challenged, by teachers who care about them . . . who want them to succeed.

★ The worst thing we can do for our children is to do nothing.

★ The future health and vitality of our society depends on our ability to properly educate our children, to guarantee that they have the skills, the confidence, and the opportunity to reach their full potential, to become full participants in our democracy.

★ I am committed—first, last, and always—to protecting the children of New York City.

★ Our children deserve the very best, and we can't be afraid of innovation in our search for the very best.

★ The challenges New York City faces in the future are clear: We must continue to make our city safer, to improve its quality of life, to expand its economy so that our children have jobs and opportunities.

★ We must have the courage and the vision to look beyond "conventional wisdom," to ignore the naysayers and to pursue our shared objectives, and to make New York City an even better place for the next generation.

From a 1996 ceremony honoring outstanding high school students:

★ As our world becomes more and more sophisticated, we must ensure that our children have the ability to lead our country into a competitive role in the coming century.

★ We must not be afraid of new ideas, especially when they have the potential to enrich and educate our children.

Promoting HealthStat, a plan to provide health coverage to uninsured New Yorkers:

★ A healthy child is a better student.

★ Schools should be the last place where children are at risk from violence or abuse.

★ We must make restoring safety in the schools a top priority, because children cannot learn when they are afraid—nor can teachers teach in a classroom ruled by fear.

★ Everyone wants the best for their child, and it should come as no surprise that poor parents want the same opportunity that wealthier families sometimes take for granted—the ability to send their child to the school of their choice, be it public, private, or parochial.

★ Every education dollar is precious.

On the New York City public school system:

★ For generations the public school classrooms of New York City have shaped great minds . . . innovators . . . artists and leaders . . . who in turn have changed the course of our nation's history.

★ A great city needs a great public school system.

★ In its greatest moments, the public school system in New York City trains all of its children to enter into our democracy, enter into our economy, and outperform the rest of the country.

★ A great schools chancellor must manage; a great schools chancellor must also inspire.

In April 1999, on his ongoing attempts to reform the school system:

★ This is a debate that I've been engaged in for ten years. It's about the good of the children, and it's only about the good of the children.

On the Board of Education, in 1995:

★ I don't think they have the foggiest idea of what they're doing, and it's a tragedy.

In January 2000, on being asked if he could move ahead with the sale of the Board of Education's dilapidated Brooklyn headquarters without the board's approval:

★ Damn right we can.

★ I was serious about that. That was not a joke. We are going to sell that damn building.

★ Education is 25 percent of the city's budget . . . but it's 100 percent of our city's future.

★ Every year that we delay in meaningful, strong school reform, a number of children are left behind. We must all work together to create a system that focuses first and foremost on improving the education of our children. In the twenty-first century, they deserve no less.

PART V

GIULIANI ON LIFE

★

26

Human Nature and Life

──────────── ★ ────────────

★ Nothing that is born out of fear and terror can stand in the way of courage, strength, and faith.

★ Courage is realizing that you're afraid and still acting.

★ First steps always lead the way to major breakthroughs.

★ Whatever obstacles that are placed in your way, I think the way to deal with it is to try to figure out how to make it, make it make you a better person.

★ Quality of life is not so much a destination to be reached as a direction in which to strive.

★ The way you get through tragedy is to look at the good things in life.

★ Dream, believe, plan, and work—this is the foundation for the process of change.

★ Ambition is a good thing. Ambition is what made America what it is, what made this city what it is.

★ In history, nothing is inevitable. Great events—both good and bad, noble and tragic—are caused by men and women, individuals who exert every ounce of their strength to change the world.

★ The art of growth is to take bad situations and try to extract the good things that we can out of them.

★ Life presents as many opportunities for happiness as it does for tragedy.

★ We must recognize that our relationship to one another as brother and sister goes deeper than our racial, ethnic, or religious identity, it is our common humanity, our identity as human beings.

★ Different times require different ways in which you feel like you have to act.

★ If you ask people to act better, they will.

★ You don't just say you're terrific. You've got to prove it.

★ I've always found it's more important to figure out what you want to do; then the specifics fall into place. Philosophy, orientation, direction is more important than specifics, because that's what develops the specifics.

★ Civility is a concept that's as old as the Greek democracy. And it's about the inherent respect people have to have for the rights of other people.

★ The pursuit of excellence is never-ending. . . .

★ It's true that if you want respect you have to give respect. . . .

★ I also believe that things happen in life for reasons that sometimes you only figure out afterwards.

Speaking at the United Jewish Appeal's 11th Biennial
Young Leadership Conference in March 1998:

★ When you lose confidence in your own ability to mold the future, sooner or later everything falls apart.

★ There are certain things that you just have to accept as risks in life, and then go about your life and lead it.

★ Greater expectations require you to develop new skills.

★ Day in, day out, month after month, we have to continue to improve our quality of life.

★ History is not predestined or preordained. The world of tomorrow is created by the choices we make today—choices that reflect the importance of every human being.

★ Instead of fearing change we should lead the way.

*From the mayor's 1996 Commencement Address to the
graduates of St. John's University School of Law:*

★ Do not listen to the cynics, the ones who have soured on
the profession and dismissed their ideals. That is the easy way
out. It is harder to maintain your ideals and fight for them.

★ Remember that with competition comes opportunity,
with opportunity comes reward.

★ Without courage, nothing else can really happen.

★ Freedom is about authority. Freedom is about the willingness of every single human being to cede to lawful authority a
great deal of discretion about what you do.

*From the mayor's 1998 address, "The Next Phase of
Quality of Life: Creating a More Civil City":*

★ The basic philosophy of quality of life requires that we
constantly move on to new areas of improvement while maintaining the gains we've already made.

★ It's the obligation of society to say that if you want to
express yourself creatively, you must do so within the context
of other people's rights.

★ When you make very little improvement and expect little
of yourself, you tend to settle for whatever single improvement
you can get. But when you believe that your work is never
done, achievements aren't reasons to rest or be satisfied.
Achievements are proof that we can make a difference, and
they make it incumbent on us all to go forward and do more.

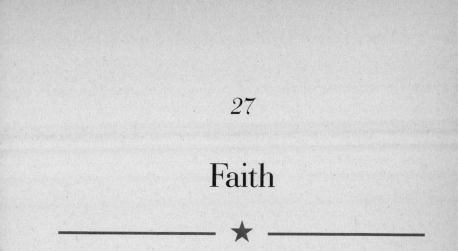

27

Faith

Raised Catholic, Giuliani considered the priesthood before deciding to pursue a career in law.

★ God has given me a lot.

When asked in May 2000 by a reporter if he felt closer to God following his cancer diagnosis, Giuliani replied:

★ Do I feel closer to God? I hope He's closer to me.

★ I've always believed that . . . God has a hand in who He allows to be here and be there and we're probably not going to know the purpose of it until after we're dead. . . . You have to do the best you can to live up to that.

Following the September 11 attacks:

★ Some of those on the highest floors lived, some of them died. Some of the firemen who went up the stairs lived. Some of them died. All those on the west side when the towers collapsed died. All those on the east lived. You have to believe God has a plan.

★ There's no question that somehow, some way all of this is part of a divine plan and you just do the best you can. And even if you felt tired or you felt depressed or you felt despondent you have to . . . just keep going.

Larry King asked Giuliani how his Catholic faith influences his role as mayor.

★ When you make a decision . . . if you are a mayor, a governor, a president, a senator, whatever, you make lots of decisions that overlap between politics and morals. And I don't think you ever know how much your religious upbringing, your religious training, affects the decisions that you make. . . . I was brought up a Catholic. And I'm sure, in subtle ways, it affects a lot of the things that I decide.

Asked by Barbara Walters in December 2001 if he believes in destiny, Giuliani answered, "I believe in God."

28

Baseball

★

★ I'm a Yankee fan. I have been a Yankee fan since I'm four. I am going to continue to be a Yankee fan. . . .

★ I love to play baseball, I love to watch baseball, I love to talk about baseball, I love to read about it.

★ And my first experience was seeing Joe DiMaggio play center field for the New York Yankees. And from then, it was just a pure love affair.

On growing up a Yankee fan in a neighborhood full of Dodger fans:

★ I became a Yankee fan in Brooklyn, which is hard to believe, right?

★ I could see the lights from my bedroom of Ebbets Field and I could hear the cheering. And my heart was in the Bronx at Yankee Stadium.

★ Exactly one mile from Ebbets Field I was born, and my father came from Manhattan, my mother from Brooklyn, and my mother required my father to live in Brooklyn, so his revenge on my mother and her entire family was to put me in Yankee pinstripes before I knew any better. And I was sent down to play with the other kids in Brooklyn, all of whom were Dodger fans and they threw me right in the mud.

★ I kept telling them, "I'm a Yankee fan, I'm gonna stay a Yankee fan." To my father it was a joke. Put a Yankee uniform on the kid, and it'll irritate all my friends and relatives and it'll be fun. But to me it was like being a martyr—"I'm not gonna give up my religion. You're not going to change me."

★ Several times they tried to assassinate me. You think I'm kidding. I'm not kidding. It's true.

★ I had to stand up for being a Yankee fan.

★ Wearing this hat in the shadow of Ebbets Field back in the early 1950s for a little kid was really tough. You used to get thrown down, yelled at, thrown in the mud, so I guess I developed this fierce spirit of rooting for the Yankees. My individuality was involved in the pinstripes. And I loved the team.

During a 1996 playoff game at Yankee Stadium, Giuliani raved:

★ No place in America has this kind of excitement. You can't match this.

★ You can't underestimate the value of baseball to the American psyche.

Speaking in April 1999 at Joe DiMaggio's memorial service:

★ He helped to create and build the pride of the Yankees and he helped to create and build the unique spirit of New York City.

★ Too often we wait until occasions like this, when our heroes have passed away, to express our love and appreciation for their efforts.

★ Just like I will always remember the first time I saw Joe DiMaggio, in the bright sunlight of center field at Yankee Stadium, I will always remember the last time I saw him, at last year's Old-Timers' Day.

An elated Giuliani describes the excitement in New York during October 2000, which saw the first Subway Series in forty-four years:

★ This has been the kind of month that makes you feel truly blessed to live in New York, the greatest and most exciting city in the world.

★ I'm smiling because this is probably one of the greatest times in sports for the city of New York. We haven't had a Subway Series in forty-four years. This is going to be absolutely terrific for New York sports fans. So here in New York, we are very, very happy and we hope the rest of the country enjoys watching it.

★ The 2000 Subway Series was a fitting symbol of the process of renewal that our city has undergone over the past seven years. The pride is back, and our city's tradition of excellence has been restored. Everyone in this city—supporters of each of our two champion teams—can once again unite under one banner, because we all live in the baseball capital of the world, and we are all proud to call ourselves New Yorkers.

★ When I ran for mayor in 1993, I made a campaign promise to bring another Subway Series to New York City. I was kidding, of course. Then in recent years, as the Yankees started to become dominant and as the Mets started to get much better, I would say that the one promise I hadn't fulfilled was a Subway Series. Well, now we've fulfilled it. And I'm glad the people of this city, many of whom were too young to experience the last Subway Series in the 1950s, have now had the experience I had as a child. And I know they'll never forget it.

On the June 2001 return of minor league baseball to Brooklyn:

★ And to have baseball back in Brooklyn has got to be one of the most wonderful things that's happened for me while I've been the mayor of New York City.

In June 2001, rejoicing in the return of minor league baseball to Coney Island:

★ This will do for Coney Island what Disney did for 42nd Street in Times Square. Take that from the mayor who's done more to economically revive New York City than any mayor in fifty years.

Praising the New York Yankees' November 2001 World Series performance:

★ New York is proud of this team. They gave us a great October, a great November, and their comebacks were hard to believe.

★ The Yankees are absolute miracle workers.

On allowing children, including his own, to skip school to attend New York Yankees' victory ticker-tape parades:

★ I get in trouble for this every year . . . Yeah, I think it's okay. Baseball can be an educational experience. Teachers and parents should use it for educational purposes. . . . Have classes come and see the parade, and have them write an essay about it.

★ Yes, I played hooky to play baseball, and somehow I survived it and became mayor.

Trying to carry on following the September 11 attacks, as he urged others, Giuliani found some solace in the New York Yankees' success.

★ I've tried to read books and go to the movies but this is the only thing that works. The only thing that has been able to divert me—and maybe there is something wrong with me—is baseball.

29

The Law

─────────── ★ ───────────

★ I'm a lawyer. I was trained to be a lawyer. It's the thing I spent most of my life doing—most for the government, some of it in private practice. And I enjoy the law, I think it brings something to human society. . . . It's the way in which we protect each other and we allow people to be creative.

★ I'm coming from a very simple place. It's called the law. Everybody has to follow it. Everybody will be dealt with in precisely the same way if they don't, and I'm going to work hard for every single person in this city, irrespective of race, religion, ethnic background.

★ There are thousands of subtle ways that we interact with the law every day. Whether it is better law enforcement that has helped make the city a safer place or civil rights protections or the Bill of Rights, we learn valuable lessons, and help shape the system through our participation.

★ I am a basically simple person. I think there are rules . . . you have to try to live as best you can by those rules. If those rules are laws, you had better darn well live by them.

On the indictment of Philippines president Marcos and his wife, October 1988:

★ I think it sends a very, very powerful and very positive signal, that this is a country where the law is paramount and no matter who you are, whether you're an American official no matter how high you are, or a foreign official, if you violate American law in a very serious way, you're just not going to get away with it, that the law is paramount for all of us. We all have to serve it.

On children and the law:

★ The failure to pay child support is not just illegal, it is morally reprehensible.

★ Priorities mean a lot in law enforcement: where you put your people, how you focus it, who you have working together.

★ Civility is about the responsibility you have as a public official and a citizen. You have to work. You have to obey laws. You have to consider the rights of others.

On the legal system's tendency to defend perpetrators, not victims of crime:

★ During the fifties and sixties, we socialized the responsibility for crime. We broke down the line between explanation and excuses, and explanations became excuses.

On holding individuals responsible for crime:

★ For purposes of ethics and of law, we elevate human beings by holding them responsible. Ultimately, you diminish human individuality and importance when you say, "Oh, well, you're not really responsible for what you did. Your parents are responsible for it, or your neighborhood is responsible for it, or society is responsible for it." In fact, if you harm another human being, you're responsible for that.

★ During my years with the federal government, I've spent lots of time in courthouses. I have seen that the real heart of a courthouse is not the structure itself but the people who work and serve the cause of justice. Whether the courthouse is old or new, it's the people who work there who do the difficult and demanding job of assuring that justice is firm and even-handed.

Giuliani played a different role in the courtroom when, in September 1999, he was selected to serve on jury duty, a first for a New York City mayor.

★ Jury duty is one of the few things that you're asked to do in exchange for living in a democracy, a government of laws. So I hope it is a message to people that this is something they should look forward to.

★ I was surprised but gratified and very honored to serve and am actually looking forward to it after all these years of being a trial lawyer.

On abortion:

★ I'm pro-choice.

★ A woman's right of choice has to be protected, and it has to be protected completely. . . .

On gay rights:

★ I'm pro–gay rights.

★ People can agree or disagree with the way someone lives their life, but they shouldn't be treated unfairly.

★ You can disagree with a person's lifestyle, but America is best when we're tolerant of each other.

On teaching children tolerance:

★ We should teach tolerance and respect, but we should do it with materials that are sensible. We don't have to get into artificial insemination at seven years old.

On his 1999 plan to have the homeless work in exchange for their shelter:

★ I think this is the highest form of compassion and love to help people to help themselves, to get them to the point where they can take care of themselves.

★ No one should have to choose between food and warmth.

★ Streets do not exist in civilized cities for the purpose of people sleeping there.

30

Cancer and Mortality

─────────── ★ ───────────

*On April 27, 2000, Giuliani announced at a press
conference that he had been diagnosed with prostate cancer.
His father died of the disease in 1981 at the age of seventy-
three.*

★ I was diagnosed yesterday with prostate cancer. It's a treatable form of prostate cancer.

★ I announced it to the press, I announced it to my family,
and I announced it to my friends. I had a big town hall meeting. I got through an hour and a half of questioning. And I was
my same old self. I lay down to bed and then I couldn't go to
sleep. And I started thinking about which treatment option,
am I going to make it, why do I have cancer, why did it happen
to me? I met with a lot of doctors and talked to them. You're
kind of in a fog. It took about a week to really come to some
kind of peace with it and decide on a course of action that
made sense for me.

To a reporter, after announcing his cancer diagnosis:

★ Pray for me.

Reflecting on the 1981 death of his father from prostate cancer:

★ It brings up very painful memories. I miss my father every day of my life. He's a very, very important reason for why I'm standing here as the mayor of New York City.

Not even the mayor's personal health could escape the watchful eye of reporters, one of whom saw Giuliani enter a hospital for testing.

★ A reporter saw me going in and figured out I was there for a prostate test. I thought it would be better to reveal what I know of it.

On the privacy of his cancer diagnosis:

★ And the focus that I'm going to have now is going to be fighting cancer, making a decision about my treatment. I'm not going to give daily updates about it, and I'm not going to deal with it as a political matter, I'm going to deal with it clearly and completely as a personal matter.

Giuliani, the tough prosecutor, faced one of his toughest battles with cancer.

★ I thought the decision about treatment would be made . . . like I've made lots of other decisions in my life, some of them real tough, none like this.

★ And I didn't realize that this involves much deeper parts of you than when you decide on how you're going to readjust your budget or how you're going to decrease taxes or what political position you're going to take . . . even the decisions I used to make as a lawyer in court . . . how are you going to argue a case or are you going to object or not? It's a much more difficult decision that starts to involve what you're about as a person.

★ I kind of approached it as if this was a big case, or a budget decision . . . [it] involves thinking about your life, mortality, the quality of your life.

On balancing his initial hormone therapy to treat prostate cancer and mayoral duties, August 2000:

★ And then every fourth to fifth day I feel a little extra fatigue, but for me that means a fourteen-hour day instead of an eighteen-hour day.

While undergoing radiation treatment for prostate cancer, fall 2000:

★ I'm not the way . . . exactly the way I'd like to be. I mean, I don't have the same amount of energy I used to have. Late in the afternoon I have to take a nap. Sometimes I can't do certain things that I want to do because I don't have the energy to do it. But I am assured by the doctors that this is temporary, and that as soon as the radiation is over and the rest of the treatment is over, the rest of my energy will return. By the same token, I don't think most people can notice it.

★ And it seemed to me, from all the analysis I did, given my own life and how I want to live it, that I would rather put up with the problems that radiation caused rather than going through the operation, the recuperation period, some of the effects of invasive surgery, but that is a very personal decision.

★ I'm on my way to a cure.

★ There are good days and bad days going through this radiation therapy, but mostly it's good.

Talking to ABC News's Diane Sawyer in January 2001 about his progress in battling prostate cancer:

★ You have to be optimistic. You got to trust your doctors, you got to decide on the treatment that you want. And then you've got to remain optimistic. You can beat cancer. You shouldn't let it frighten you too much.

★ I got very good advice from my doctors; they mapped out the whole thing, nothing unexpected. And I had some friends who had gone through it, different forms of treatment. And I get the chance, now, to counsel a lot of people, so I try to give them the benefit of the advice that I got. . . . You get very frightened of it at first, then you realize you can deal with it. It takes a little while though.

On being asked by Today *show's Matt Lauer about his health, June 2001:*

★ My health is doing well. I went through a difficult time with prostate cancer . . . went through radiation treatment, hormone treatment. And right now things are looking really, really well, and I thank God for that.

On being asked by Barbara Walters during a December 2001 20/20 appearance if, following his cancer diagnosis, he thought he was going to die:

★ I don't really think I had ever accepted my own mortality . . . thought about death as a realistic thing until then.

Assuring eighteen-year-old Yonatan Barnik at Shaare Zedek hospital during his December 2001 trip to Israel:

★ I have overcome cancer; so will you.

On life and politics following his cancer diagnosis:

★ You see politics differently. You see life differently.

★ When you face something like that, it changes you; you have a better sense of the meaning of life.

★ Just the contemplation of it makes you think about what's important in life.

★ You look at life very, very differently. You see the value of it. You see the value of every day. I think, ultimately, you appreciate it more.

Talking with NBC News's Tim Russert after announcing his cancer diagnosis:

★ I think things do happen for a reason. And I don't think I'll know the reason for this for a few years, but at some point, hopefully, I'll be able to figure out why this all happened and how it happened. I can already see some good things that have come out of it.

★ I tend to think now that love is more important than I thought it was. I think about all the love that I've received and it's amazing. . . . I've gotten thousands of letters giving me support, giving me love. And I think about the people that have to face this alone, without this incredibly large system of support and encouragement, and it has to be terrible.

★ And I guess because I've been in public life so long and politics, I used to think the core of me was in politics, probably. It isn't. When you feel your mortality and your humanity, you realize that the core of you is, first of all, being able to take care of your health and make sure . . . that you're in good health, and to deal with a disease like cancer in the most effective way possible so you can be useful to the people that you really care about and really care about you.

★ I think I understand myself a lot better. I think I understand what's important to me better. Maybe I'm not completely there yet; I would be foolish to think that I was in a few weeks. But I think I'm heading in that direction.

★ I've also found in thinking about it, suffering over it, that something—it's very painful and very difficult—but something very beautiful happens. It makes you figure out what you're really all about and what's really important to you and what should be important to you—you know, what, where the core of you really exists.

★ There's no question that if you confront not just cancer, if you confront your mortality directly, however you get to confront it, you're going to become a different person. But I don't think you become a different person in thirty days. I think a process takes place, and somehow you remain yourself, and then something happens to you. Something good or bad can happen to you, depending on how you use it and what you do with it, and what I'm determined to do is to have it make me a better person, make me understand myself better, the people around me better, and where my first, second, third obligations are.

In September 2000:

★ I want to again thank all of the people that have helped me, assisted me, all of them that have given me support, particularly people who have dealt with prostate cancer and other forms of cancer, who come up to me at parades, at rallies, when I am playing golf, and explain to me what they have been through, and it really helps a lot. It helps to elucidate what is best for you. And I also feel that in that way you can give something back to other people and give them some advice about how they can handle this and deal with it. I am very fortunate to have a lot of people that help me and support me. And I feel very bad for people who don't have that support system.

Encouraging others diagnosed with cancer:

★ Don't be afraid of cancer. It's curable, it's treatable, and it can be dealt with, if you deal with it. And you take the tests that are necessary to detect it at an early stage, spend the time to do that, whether it's prostate cancer, breast cancer, or any form of cancer, and then put yourself in the hands of responsible physicians, of which there are many, particularly in the city of New York, and then deal with it.

★ Your first reaction is going to be the horrible word *cancer*. You are going to be very frightened. You're going to be very upset. You are going to have some nights in which you are sleeping and you get up and see yourself dead and you think your life is over. Then you are going to start realizing that the therapies are becoming much more effective, and the best thing to do is, in a very positive way, get involved and have a very positive attitude about it.

★ If you have a disease you can cure, thank God. And if you don't, there's nothing you can do about it. You have to conduct your life, take reasonable precautions, and not shut yourself down.

PART VI

GIULIANI ON LIFE AFTER SEPTEMBER 11

★

31

Thoughts on Life After September 11

———————— ★ ————————

★ You realize after something like September 11, that life is very, very short and very precious....

Speaking at the September 23 memorial service for victims of the September 11 attacks held at Yankee Stadium:

★ There are no politics here. It's about being an American. Not a Democrat. Not a Republican. All those little ideologies, all those little fights we have, they don't mean anything. We're all together. We need to rely on each other. We need to help each other. We need to fight back. We need to prevail.

★ By reflecting on it and understanding what happened to us, we're going to be even stronger.

At the wedding of Diane Gorumba and police officer Michael Ferrito, just days after the World Trade Center attacks, Giuliani fulfilled his promise to walk Diane down the aisle after her brother Michael, a firefighter, had died in the line of duty in August.

★ This is what life is all about. You have to go on and take advantage of the good things in life.

★ I'm trying to get the city—and I think it's succeeding—to focus on the good parts of life.

★ You go through five weeks like this and you realize that the strength that you have largely comes from what your mother and father taught you.

★ You have every right to be scared. But the reality is that we can live through it. Courage is realizing that you're afraid and still acting.

★ Maybe after having gone through all the death and all the pain of September 11 and the aftermath of it all, you put life in perspective.

On grieving:

★ You just have to let whatever feelings you have come out and do the best you can to process it all.

★ We have to learn how to grieve and how to enjoy ourselves in the same day. Maybe that's a lesson for life, not just for now.

★ I try to tell people, "The only thing you can do is talk about it." You can't keep it inside. You got to get it out.

Talking with Oprah Winfrey about guiding friends and family of September 11 victims who may be facing death for the first time:

★ I'm an eternal optimist, so I think going through this is going to make them tougher. They'll be able to face the rest of their lives better—but it's going to take awhile to get there, and it won't be true for everyone.

★ We must go on living our lives with strength, courage, and a resolve to not allow fear to compromise our freedom or our way of life.

Advice to parents discussing the events of September 11 with their children:

★ They should be honest with them. Honest in a sensitive and a careful way. Honest about what happened, why it happened. I think you should be honest with children. I think they need to know the enormity of this, how difficult it is, how much pain, how much suffering is going to be caused by it. And then I think they need to learn the history of America, and why it's necessary to go through this. . . . Don't hide things from them. Explain what has happened to them. But explain the importance of their way of life. Explain the importance of democracy and the rule of law, and regard for human beings, and the kinds of things that are under attack right now.

★ You see that the human spirit has survived the worst attack that anyone could have imagined. And is maybe in a certain sense even strengthened by it.

On being asked by a caller on Larry King Live *how the weeks following September 11 had affected him emotionally or changed his way of life:*

★ All these things that happen to you, I don't know if they really change you. They . . . give you more depth. . . . of your understanding of human nature . . . to your understanding of the value of life and how you have to live it.

On being asked by ABC News's Barbara Walters in the days following the September 11 attacks if he was "a changed man":

★ When I went through prostate cancer, I was, therefore, a changed man. I changed for a while, then I went back to the way I was. I don't know if you really change. I think you grow. I don't think I'd be able to handle this at all if it weren't for the things that happened to me in my past. You keep growing, you keep changing, you keep, hopefully, expanding. And I haven't had the time in less than a week that's gone by to actually figure out about changing. I'm just doing what I think I have to do to try to get the city through this and participate in helping to get the country through it.

Asked by Oprah Winfrey if he is a better person following the events of September 11, Giuliani replied, "I hope so. I understand the value of life a lot better."

Giuliani spent Christmas Day serving meals to rescue workers cleaning up the World Trade Center disaster area.

★ There's still mourning. We're still very, very hurt and very sorrowful, and we'll always be, for the people we love, that we lost. But I think we're a much stronger group of people today than we were on September 10. We're spiritually much more united, and this holiday season is one that we're embracing, maybe with even more enthusiasm than we usually do.

32

"America's Mayor" Finds Time to Grieve

———————— ★ ————————

On being asked by Barbara Walters whom he relies on for comfort in the wake of September 11:

★ I lean on some of the best people that any mayor ever had working with him or for him or around him.

Giuliani reflecting with Newsweek's *Jonathan Alter on his first public display of emotion following September 11:*

★ I thought it was good to let people know you're just going to cry . . . It's okay. You gotta cry.

On being asked by CBS News's anchor Jane Clayson how the events of September 11 had affected him:

★ I lost some very, very good friends from the police department, the fire department. Barbara Olson and Ted Olson are very close friends of mine. It's going to affect me, I think, the way it will affect thousands of other New Yorkers, who . . . will find that they lost people that they knew there.

"America's Mayor" on coping with the September 11 attacks:

★ The whole experience continues to be very strange because it is very personal, but it's also part of my public duty as mayor to deal with it.

Giuliani recalled encountering friend Ray Downey, NYFD battalion chief, leading the rescue effort at the base of the World Trade Center on the morning of the attacks. Downey was one of several firefighters killed that morning.

★ So I wave to him, not thinking I am saying good-bye. No way.

Giuliani managed to take a quick walk through a tunnel under the FDR Drive toward the East River, while leading rescue efforts September 13 and reflecting on the tragedy that had engulfed his city.

★ I wanted to look at it. I wanted to look at the river. It was still there. I looked at the skyline. It was still there.

On the September 11 deaths of NYCFD Chaplain Father Mychal Judge, First Deputy Commissioner Bill Fehan, and Chief of Department Peter Ganci:

★ This is a horrible, horrible tragedy. These were wonderful men. They were the leadership of our fire department.

Speaking at the funeral of NYFD Chief of Department Peter Ganci:

★ You have to pay a big price for democracy. And now we're learning what that means. It means we have to sustain these losses; we have to have the strength to get through it.

Following the attacks:

★ The feelings that I had yesterday I think I'll be thinking about for the rest of my life. I lost some very, very good friends, people that I know very, very well, personal friends, and talked to some of them just a few minutes before they died.

On being asked by Hardball's *Chris Matthews to describe his emotions throughout September 11:*

★ I don't know that I'll . . . in my entire lifetime, be able to really adequately describe what my emotions were.

At the funeral service for New York City Fire Department captain Terence Hatton, husband of Giuliani's executive assistant, Beth Petrone-Hatton:

★ I've known many, many fine men in my life, and eulogized too many . . . Terry Hatton really stood out. . . . He is the kind of man I would like my son to grow up and become.

Beth Petrone-Hatton learned she was pregnant September 21. Amid all the suffering, Giuliani remarked, "That's the best news I've had."

On the overwhelming number of funerals and services for emergency personnel killed in the World Trade Center attacks:

★ I can't go to every funeral. I can't go to every wake . . . I try to go to as many as possible but I can't go to all of them, and it's killing me and the fire commissioner.

On being asked by Oprah Winfrey about the first time he cried following the September 11 tragedy:

★ The first night I went home . . . when I went home and turned on the TV, I saw shots of the buildings coming down. I just sat there and cried. I said to myself, "Thank God no one is around." You feel like you can't do that—cry—because you're supposed to be in charge. But I remember telling myself at one point that I would give myself room to cry, because crying is a sign of strength.

When asked by A&E's Harry Smith if he had a chance to grieve in the weeks after September 11, Giuliani replied, "Intermittently."

33

Looking Back: Reflecting on His Time as Mayor

★

Giuliani's tenure as mayor was the longest job he ever held, eight years.

★ This was the most stability in my life, being mayor.

Giuliani knew the time would come to leave the job he loved, as he looked ahead in 1998.

★ There's a two-term limit on the mayor of New York City. I need a job when I'm finished.

In 1998, he reflected on what he may do after his term.

★ I really haven't started imagining what I'm going to do after I'm done being mayor. I used to think I'd like to run the Metropolitan Opera House, or manage the Yankees—but Joe Torre is doing such a good job that nobody's ever going to be able to follow him as manager. So I really have not given serious thought to what do I do afterward.

Giuliani proposed a three-month extension of his term to ease the transition to a new administration following the September 11 attacks.

★ So a lengthy, sensible, thoughtful, careful transition will cure a problem that exists anyway—a problem that's made more severe by the situation that we're in. It will give people in the city with fears about what's going to happen a certain sense of confidence.

On being asked by CNN anchor Paula Zahn if he would pursue legislation to seek a third term as mayor:

★ My desire is to try to unify the city, not create a source of division.

★ This was an absolutely great job.

★ For the past eight years I've had the honor of serving as the mayor of my hometown, the capital of the world.

★ It seemed to me that what I had to do was to totally change the direction and course of New York City. Maybe I was right about that, maybe I was wrong about it. But that's the way I felt I had to operate.

★ I honestly think I did the best I could. I'm a human being, I have limitations.

★ I tried very hard to do this job 100 percent. I devoted myself to it.

★ The pursuit of excellence is never over—for individuals or a city—but to a greater extent than I ever imagined, we have accomplished what we set out to do.

★ In ways both big and small, our lives are better than they were eight years ago.

★ I worked as hard as I could for the people of the city. I feel enormously proud at the fact that I was able to represent them. I thank them very much for that opportunity.

★ Any kind of assessment of what kind of mayor I am right now is unfair. I don't mean unfair to me; I mean unfair historically. The assessment should be made at least a couple of years from now.

★ As mayor, I used to always feel the important thing is that people respect me, not love me—but it is really much nicer when they love you, too. I'm going to try to keep it that way.

★ I've given every effort I am capable of trying to do as good a job of mayor as I could possibly do.

★ People saw from Septmber 11 on that I worked equally hard for all the people of the city, and I worked harder for the people who needed it. I think most people understand that I relate to New Yorkers. . . .

★ The degree of ethnic, racial, and religious tension in this city on September 10 was considerably less than it was eight years earlier or back in 1989 when I first ran for mayor. Polls would actually show that.

★ Perhaps most people understand that I relate to people as New Yorkers. I don't see minorities; everyone is a minority. Nobody is the majority in New York City. It hasn't been that way for a long time. I treat everybody equally. Everyone was treated the same way, with respect, unless they show they don't deserve it.

★ It seemed to me that what I had to do was to totally change the direction and course of New York City. Maybe I was right about that, maybe I was wrong about it, but that's the way I felt I had to operate. I saw this city deteriorating. . . . I saw the city on the front page of *Time* magazine in 1990 in which the front cover said "New York City: The Rotting Apple."

Barbara Walters asked Giuliani in December 2001 what he is proudest of as mayor.

★ Reestablishing the spirit of the city is the thing I'm the proudest of. . . . When I came into office the spirit of New York City was depressed and didn't believe in itself. And my mayoralty was to make people believe in the city of New York again. Otherwise they never could have gotten through September 11.

*Giuliani cited his unsuccessful attempts to abolish the
Board of Education as his only regret upon leaving office.*

★ We were not able to bring about the reform that I would
like for one simple reason—because we couldn't convince the
State Legislature to do away with the Board of Education and
give me control of the educational system.

★ I think that the biggest regret that I have is schools.

*Giuliani deemed his deputy mayors and commissioners "the
most talented group that has ever served in city
government."*

*Giuliani summed up his relationship with the media in his
final sit-down interview with reporters.*

★ You in the press spend a great deal of time figuring out the
things I do wrong. I always figured I should reserve myself for
the more positive approach to things. I don't approach life that
way. I realize that you make mistakes. Maybe it comes from
having been a baseball player. If you make an error, if you
spend your time thinking about the error, you make another
one.

34

Preparing to
Say Good-bye:
Final Days in Office

━━━━━━━━━━━━ ★ ━━━━━━━━━━━━

Following his last Thanksgiving Day Parade as mayor:

★ I don't know really how to describe it. There are times when I feel very emotional about it. Yesterday, two or three times during the parade, when I saw the large crowds and I saw how enthusiastic they were, I think there probably was a little tear in my eye one or two times, although I usually try to hide it.

★ I've never been more proud of our city. I've never been more proud to be a New Yorker, and it has been a great honor to serve as your mayor.

★ I feel a tremendous amount of excitement. I feel the excitement of . . . what's on the other side of the mountain. . . . I feel like I've done everything I can do.

★ Sure, it is going to be very difficult leaving this job. I love it. It's not a job, this is a full-time, twenty-four-hour-a-day relationship with the people of the city of New York. At the same time I have the feeling that you have when you feel you've done everything you can do.

★ I have the feeling that you have when you've done everything you can do, where you feel, "Well, I haven't held back any effort." There are things probably I would do differently in terms of judgments I would make if I could make them again, but I've given every effort that I'm capable of and tried to do as good a job as mayor as I possibly could do. So I feel happy about that at least.

★ I think at some point along the way I came to peace with the idea that my term is over, and you gotta move on to the next phase.

On leaving office, Giuliani says, "There's no sadness at all."

★ After September 11, and when you see what real sadness is, it puts it all in perspective.

★ I'm quite satisfied with the fact that it has to end. I've done this job longer than any job I've ever done in my life, eight years, and it's about time to pass it on to someone else.

★ Maybe it's because of what happened on September 11. I realize that things end—whether it's being mayor or your life—it ends. And part of being able to handle life is being able to handle the changes that take place.

Giuliani said he is "at peace" with his departure.

On leaving office with high approval ratings:

★ I just better get out of here quick.

Enjoying continual warm welcomes from New Yorkers in his final days in office:

★ It's a wonderful feeling. I feel like all the hard work we did is appreciated, and it's great. It's really great.

Giuliani went on to say:

★ It is the source of a lot of strength.

Three days before leaving office, Giuliani announced tentative agreements to build new retractable-roof stadiums for the New York Yankees and Mets, requiring the approval of Mayor-elect Michael Bloomberg.

★ This is a tremendous economic investment for the city. Neither of these stadiums would require any new taxes. This is the way you build a city—this is how we can keep New York growing.

★ You can't underestimate the effect on civic pride and the economy of the city.

★ The last thing in the world we want to do now in the light of what has happened to us since September 11 is take a step back. This is a very good deal for the city of New York.

From his final City Hall press conference:

★ I think that if you're the mayor of New York City, you get used to the fact that you're going to have a very emotional relationship with the people of the city and the press. I'll have very, very warm memories of all the battles that I had in this room. I enjoyed them. It was like being in court.

★ I am going to miss the interchange. I thought it was very, very valuable and very important and I really think it had a lot more to do with the spirit of the city than many people realized.

★ I think I've gotten fair treatment—most of the time.

Final thoughts on the September 11 attacks:

★ The mourning and grief and sorrow that emanates from that attack is not over by any means, and maybe will never be over.

★ America emerged stronger from September 11, but it will only continue to be strong if we remain dedicated to our principles as Americans. I hope this spirit of unity and patriotism will grow rather than dissipate as we move further away from the horrible events of that day.

On his last day in office, Giuliani spoke at a graduation ceremony for probationary firefighters and remembered those lost in the September 11 attacks.

★ Here they delivered the biggest blow ever to an American city . . . and your brothers raised the American flag—high, tall, and strong. At that moment I knew that no matter how long it would take, we would win the war against terrorism.

Giuliani was selected as Time *magazine's Person of the Year, December 2001. Giuliani says of the award:*

★ I was very humbled, and very moved, by the selection.

★ I believe the people of New York were selected as the people of the year.

★ I got all the credit resting on the shoulders of these people that have had one of the most heroic three months I think any people have ever had.

★ I was stunned, a little. It was really strange. It's hard to think of yourself that way.

★ I feel that this award is intended for all of the people of New York who defended the spirit of America and have helped to make the American spirit stronger than it's ever been before. And by the people of New York, I mean the people of America.

★ There's no question that the only reason that I was selected the person of the year is that the people of New York are the people of the year. There is no question about it.

At a news conference following the award announcement, Giuliani discussed how the editors of Time *magazine were considering naming Osama bin Laden Person of the Year.*

★ I think it's much better that I was selected as a representative of the people of New York City rather than him. His ultimate objective was obviously not just to kill people, his objective was to destroy the spirit of America. The spirit of America is now stronger than it has ever been before.

Mayor Giuliani delivered his Farewell Address December 27, 2001. "America's Mayor" was four days from leaving office after having served for eight years.

★ Although I have to leave you as the mayor, soon I resume the much more honorable title of citizen, citizen of New York and citizen of the United States. You get to be mayors and council members and congressmen and senators and governors and even presidents for short periods of time, but you always remain a citizen.

Giuliani used the site of his address, St. Paul's Chapel, as a symbol of the strength of the American people; although just two blocks from the World Trade Center, it is still standing.

★ The place where George Washington prayed when he first became president of the United States stood strong, powerful, untouched, undaunted by the attacks of these people who hate what we stand for. Because what we stand for is so much stronger than they are.

★ It doesn't matter if you came here rich or poor, if you came here voluntarily or involuntarily, if you came here in freedom or in bondage. All that matters is that you embrace America and understand its ideals and what it's all about.

★ We're not one race, we're many; we're not one ethnic group, we're everyone; we're not one language, we're all of these people. So what ties us together? We're tied together by our belief in political democracy. We're tied together by our belief in religious freedom. We're tied together by our belief in capitalism, a free economy where people make their own choices about the spending of their money. We're tied together because we respect human life. We're tied together because we respect the rule of law. Those are the group of ideas that make us Americans.

★ I think the key to our success as a city, the reason we are the most famous city in the world, and the reason why we really legitimately are the capital of the world, is really just one thing: immigration. We are an open city. We have never been afraid of people. We've never been afraid of people no matter what their color, religion, ethnic background. We're a city in which our diversity is our greatest strength.

★ There are just too many things to talk about and too many people to thank. But there is one big change that has taken place that's the most important and the one that I wanted to bring about. And that one I'm really sure of. It's a change in the spirit of the city. That city that used to be the rotting apple, that 60, 70, 80 percent of the people wanted to leave and nobody wanted to come to, that city now is very strong and it is a confident city. It's a city that has withstood the worst attack of any city in America or in the history of America and people are standing up as tall, as strong, and as straight as this church.

★ So please remember that my strength completely comes from you. It isn't me, it is yours. And you are going to keep it. And the city is going to go on. And it's going to be a great, great city.

35

Passing the Torch

———————— ★ ————————

On NYC Mayor-elect Michael Bloomberg:

★ I'm very, very confident that the city would be in absolutely excellent hands in the hands of Mike Bloomberg.

★ If you had to go out and find the right person to handle the city when its economy has to be rebuilt, its budget has to be restructured . . . to give businesses the confidence to stay here, Mike Bloomberg is the perfect choice. He understands private business.

★ And that's the advice that I'd give to Michael. You don't have to be controversial, but you've got to stand for something. And you can't be afraid of being unpopular.

From a public endorsement of Mayor-elect Michael Bloomberg:

★ It's been an honor to be your mayor for eight years. You may not have always agreed with me, but I gave it my all. I love this city, and I'm confident it will be in good hands with Mike Bloomberg.

Leaving City Hall for the last time:

★ I walk out tonight and turn over to Mike Bloomberg a different city than the one that was handed to me.

After swearing in Bloomberg at Times Square minutes after the ball dropped and 2002 began, Giuliani urged his successor:

★ Take care of these people.

On legacies:

★ I give no thought to my legacy. I think legacies happen after you're dead, and I don't intend to die, so I don't give any thought to legacy. I think that's one of the silly things that goes on among politicians when they start thinking about legacies. You do the best you can, you do it with all the energy you have, and then you, you . . . let history and the future take care of however they view you. It's not my job to figure out my legacy.

★ I don't think you get to determine how you're remembered.

★ I get nervous about legacies. Dead people have legacies.

The outgoing mayor and lifelong Yankee fan proposed one of his own:

★ I don't know—"Most Yankees championships in a long time" could be one.

36

New York's Finest: The New York City Police and Fire Departments

———————— ★ ————————

★ The most rewarding part of being mayor of the city of New York is working with so many people who have the desire, the will, and the courage to make our city a better place. I have a profound sense of respect and love for the men and women of the police and fire departments who have worked so hard to help make our city a safer, brighter, and more beautiful place for all New Yorkers.

Speaking at a November 12, 2001, news conference following the crash of Flight 587 in Rockaway, Queens:

★ So once again, we are in the debt of our firefighters, our New York City police officers, and our Port Authority police officers, who did an absolutely magnificent job, and God bless them.

Praising the heroic bravery of firefighters and emergency personnel:

★ They do something very special . . . If you don't feel for them, I don't know who you feel for.

In December 1994, on the response of emergency personnel following an explosion on the New York City subway:

★ These people are so professional, it's really remarkable.

★ And also note the fact that the emergency response in this city, as it proves over and over again, is just about the best in the world.

On the New York City Police Department:

★ There's never been a mayor who understands the psyche of the police department the way I do.

★ The job of a police officer is difficult, it is a sacrifice, it's also an enormously rewarding one. There can be nothing that gives you more of a sense of self-worth than being able to help other people, because that's really what your job is all about.

Honoring the bravery of the NYPD:

★ Most of us walk around every day with our chest, our lungs, stomach, and heart vulnerable to the world, and thank God we don't have to think twice about it. But for police officers, every day, just in the act of putting on the vest, the thought crosses their mind that today might be the day that the vest is used.

★ They have to make decisions that I don't know that I'd be capable of making.

★ I think that cops are no different than anybody else. There are an overwhelming majority of good cops and there are a few bad ones. And then I think cops are a little different than everybody else. They put their lives at risk to save us, and that's different than most citizens in society.

★ They are the bravest. They're the best people you ever met.

★ We need police officers in the community, relating to the community and trying to prevent crimes. That's the main focus of a police officer's duty . . . should be to prevent crimes rather than having to deal with it afterwards.

In support of President Clinton's 1994 call for funding for one hundred thousand police officers as part of his crime package:

★ We do need one hundred thousand police officers throughout America and we should really do it, not pretend.

In February 1999, following the death of African immigrant Amadou Diallo, shot forty-one times by plainclothes policemen in the Bronx:

★ As we ask the police department to show more respect, and we make Herculean efforts—*they* do—to show more respect, we have something that we have a right to demand. We have a right to demand more respect from the citizens of the city for the police officers of the city of New York. It's about time to stop carrying signs pretending that they're racist, it's about time to stop carrying signs equating them to the KKK, and it's about time to stop invocations of Adolf Hitler, about our police department.

Giuliani at Diallo's funeral:

★ I'm very sorry for what happened, and I think everyone in the city is very sorry for what happened, and we wish it could be reversed in some way.

From his address at the 1999 NYPD graduation:

★ We understand that you are doing something very special, that other people may not be able to do—that many other people are not able to do: you are putting your lives at risk to protect the lives of other people. That's a very, very special person that can do that—it takes a special kind of courage, it takes a special ability to discipline your emotions and the feelings of fear. . . .

★ Ultimately, you should consider yourselves . . . civil rights workers. You protect the citizens of the city's . . . most basic right: to be free of crime and free of fear.

★ You protect the right that people have to safety because if people don't have safety they have absolutely nothing else. . . . They can't use their public spaces, they can't use their schools, they can't use their libraries.

★ And if I can give you just one piece of advice . . . when you arrest people or when you deal with people—"Yes, sir," "No, sir," "Mr.," "Mrs.," "Ms." Go out of your way to engage them in an even overly respectful way even when you're angry, even when you're afraid, even when you have every right to be angry and afraid, that's the professionalism of "Courtesy, Professionalism, and Respect." You'll protect yourself better that way and you'll engender a tremendous respect for this department—in the worst set of circumstances to act in the most respectful way possible.

★ The city goes through probably some of the worst agony and distress when we lose a police officer because we understand how important police officers are to us. . . . Police work is very, very difficult work. It's very complex work. It involves people's emotions in ways that the other work that people do really doesn't compare to it.

Responding to police criticism in 1997:

★ Find somebody else to beat up for a while, other than the police department.

On corruption:

★ Police brutality is unacceptable, it's abhorrent, it should be cut out, and it's criminal conduct. People should go to jail for it the way people should go to jail for murdering someone, beating someone, taking advantage of someone.

★ I think a brutal cop should be off the police force and in jail.

Following the 1997 torture of Haitian immigrant Abner Louima by New York City police officers in Brookyln's 70th Precinct station house:

★ If you really understand what it means to be a police officer, you will be among the most revulsed and repulsed by what happened here. If you don't understand that, you should really leave the police department.

On the New York City Police Department, July 1998:

★ Have there been situations in which police officers have acted improperly, brutally, and horribly? Yes, but so have all the other citizens of New York City and other parts of the country. Occasionally there are cops that are bad; that doesn't make all cops bad.

★ I think people realize that the major risk that you face in society, New York, or anyplace else is not from the police, it's from your fellow citizens. For one police incident, there are one thousand incidents of violence, citizen on citizen, community member on community member. We need the police to reduce that greater risk for us. But we also need the police to act respectfully and decently and lawfully. And when a cop is a criminal, that cop should be pursued the way a criminal is pursued.

In 2000, defending the NYPD on attacks of racial profiling:

★ It's part of a political game that gets played in this city, which is, "Let's see if we can work up racial tension by misunderstanding what people are saying in good faith." They do it all the time to me. I'm used to it.

Reflecting on the tragic Father's Day 2001 deaths of three NYC firefighters, Harry Ford, Brian Fahey, and John Downing, killed while fighting a five-alarm blaze in Astoria, Queens:

On the New York City Fire Department:

★ In New York City, we have a very special respect for firefighters. The heart of a great fire department is the skill, dedication, and bravery of its firefighters.

★ These tragic deaths remind us that we should never take the remarkable sacrifice of our firefighters for granted. The natural human instinct is to run away from fire. Our firefighters go into the heat and the flames and the smoke with one and only one objective—to save other people's lives. They don't ask the age, the gender, the religion, or the race of the people inside. All they want to know is whether there are human beings whose lives are at risk. That's the purest expression of love that I can imagine.

★ I can't think of a more tragic Father's Day, as eight children were suddenly left without a father.

★ Every firefighter's family understands the risks that their loved ones take when they put on the uniform of the New York City Fire Department. They hope and they pray that no harm will come to them. But that never lessens the shock or the sorrow that overwhelms a family when one of our city's bravest dies in the line of duty.

★ Their courage and determination should serve as an example to us all. When firefighters run into a burning building, they don't stop to wonder whether the people inside are rich or poor, what race they are, or what religion they practice. Their thoughts are focused solely on the individuals inside that need to be saved. Their actions represent the purest example of love for humanity.

On the performance of NYC firefighters and police officers put to the test once again in the November 2001 crash of Flight 587 in Rockaway, Queens:

★ The fire was out in two hours. It never got beyond where it originally started. It's because of their expertise, their bravery, their unbelievable ability to fight fire, which I think is unlike anybody else in the world.

Honoring the NYFD at a promotion ceremony shortly after the September 11 attacks:

★ There is no better example, none, no better example of courage than the fire department of the city of New York.

★ You're all my heroes. You have been from the time I was a little boy and from the day that I became the mayor of New York City.

Praising the efforts of the NYFD following the December 2001 five-alarm blaze at the Cathedral of Saint John the Divine:

★ They responded in four minutes. They contained a fire that could have been a catastrophe, saved lives, saved some of the most valuable property in the city of New York, this great, wonderful cathedral that is very much a part of the life of the city.

37

The Future

──────────── ★ ────────────

★ I need to take a break, reflect on everything that's happened. I haven't had enough time to think about any of this. I could use a vacation.

Upon leaving office, Giuliani planned to run a consulting firm, Giuliani Partners, with some of his top aides.

★ We're going to re-create the very close relationship and efficiency and effectiveness that we've had in government in the private sector.

On speculation that he may run for public office again:

★ These things are never planned out.

★ I think from the outside, when people look at political officials and political leaders, they think they're walking around with a big plan in their head. But by and large, you let it happen and make decisions as they come up.

★ I don't know what I'm going to be doing in 2008. I wasn't planning, when I was associate attorney general or U.S. attorney, to run for mayor. It all came gradually much closer to the time that I did it.

★ I spent my first seven and three-quarter years as mayor living out my father's advice that it's better to be respected than loved, but I had forgotten the last part of what he used to say: "Eventually, you will love me."

38

America the Beautiful

———————— ★ ————————

★ Since John Winthrop first called us "a city on the hill,"
America and especially New York City have been a beacon of
hope and decency for people in every corner of the globe.

★ Americans are not a single ethnic group. Americans are
not of one race or one religion. We are defined as Americans
by our belief in political, economic, and religious freedom,
democracy, the rule of law, and respect for human life.

★ We're a country that is very, very much a desirable place to be. Instead of being afraid of that, we should be exalted by that. We're the place that people want to come to. And we want to maintain ourselves as the place that people want to come to. We don't want to change the essential nature of what America is all about. And just because people look a little different or act a little different or talk a little different, you would think that two hundred years of history would teach us that in absorbing all of that, we become greater. And when we're afraid of all that, we kind of diminish ourselves.

★ It is, after all, our differences that have forged our unique American character of tolerance.

★ America is the greatest nation in the history of the world.

★ This is an absolutely beautiful country.

Speaking at Kennedy School of Government, October 1996:

★ A threat to immigration can be a threat to the future of our country. Just as they did in years past, immigrants today revitalize and reinvigorate the culture and economy of our cities and states.

★ The most patriotic people that we have, by and large, in our city are the people who are here new, the people who see it for the first time, who then remind us and our children that we really are lucky to be here. And that's a process that's a very real one, a very important one, and it's one that you don't want to lose.

Addressing leaders of the Cuban American National Foundation, the self-proclaimed leading anti-Castro group, October 1998:

★ A dictator who oppresses people is someone who should be ostracized by the United States.

★ Immigration is one of the best ways to increase the number of talented scientists, inventors, domestic laborers, highly skilled engineers, computer programmers, and managers. Immigrants enhance our country's competitiveness, they do not detract from it.

Praising immigrants in his weekly column, July 2001:

★ They serve as an example to us all, and remind us why we are so fortunate to call ourselves citizens of the United States.

★ Ellis Island is a wonderful place, it's a sacred place, and it's hallowed ground in American history. . . . No less than 40 percent of all Americans can trace their ancestors' arrival in the United States to Ellis Island. For these fellow citizens, Ellis Island represents the birthplace of their American dream.

★ America became the most successful nation in history because of our constant process of reevaluation, reform, and revitalization, a process that is driven by immigrants who come here to create better lives for themselves and their children. We are constantly being reinvented, not just by the free flow of ideas but by the free flow of people.

★ New York has always benefited more than any other city from not being afraid of what immigrants can bring to us. . . . Immigrants remind us of what we should be doing that we're not doing. Immigrants remind us, for example, of why we're so fortunate to be Americans because they have figured out why they want to be Americans. Some of us have forgotten why we're Americans. We think only of our problems. We don't think of all the wonderful things and opportunities that exist in this country that don't exist anyplace else. Immigrants remind us of that.

★ Ellis Island stands as one of the greatest symbols of the promise of America. Millions traveled through this gateway to make better lives for themselves and their children. They came from different backgrounds . . . they spoke different languages . . . they looked different . . . they traveled to different destinations throughout the country . . . but what united them was the belief in America and the fundamental principles of our democracy.

★ Immigrants constantly infuse new life into our economy and culture. They come with the desire to succeed, they work hard, and they challenge us to do better.

★ Our country would not be the richest, most successful nation if it were not for immigrants. From the inception of this country, the very process of immigration is what has come to define us as a nation.

★ The very best times of our history suggest we should be optimistic and see people as opportunities. The new people that come here not only make a better life for themselves but for us all.

★ One of the reasons why we are such a great country is immigrants that come here are self-starters who are often courageous and ambitious. It takes courage and drive to leave your native country and start a new life in a new land. Immigration has proven to be a powerful force for growth and progress in this country.

★ We make true progress in America when we find a way to responsibly give people more freedom, when we responsibly give them a little bit more control over their own lives; then people really surprise you and they do a great job of it.

From the mayor's "Reaching Out to All New Yorkers by Restoring Work to the Center of City Life Address," July 1998:

★ The social contract states that for every right, there is an obligation . . . for every benefit, there is a duty. That, in life, you have to give back. And when we reassert that with people, we make them better people. And we call them to something higher in themselves. And it's unimaginable and untold what they can accomplish when you do that. That's America when it's at its greatest.

★ We are constantly being reinvented by the infusion of new people and new ideas into our city and our country. This process has come to define us as a nation. It makes us who we are today.

★ Immigrants bring new ideas, new energy, and a new appreciation for American values and ideals. They challenge us to do better. We all benefit from their industry and prosperity.

★ To be able to defend democracy, you have to understand the value of democracy. You have to understand it is a very unique gift we've been given to be Americans.

★ There's nothing like America. . . . This is the only country millions of people want to come to in the whole world. That's got to tell us something about ourselves . . . tell us something about what a wonderful country this is, what a great form of government we have, what good people we are.

★ The core of what makes America a great nation is that we are *not* connected by a common racial, ethnic, or religious background but by a common belief.

★ The test of being an American is not a test of one's ethnic background, religion, or race, it's a much more fundamental test—a test of whether you truly believe that "all men are created equal." It's a test of whether you are willing to live by that principle. If you pass that test and live by that principle whether you came here a day ago or are descendants from the *Mayflower* you are an American.

★ The United States is unique in the world because its citizens are united not by a common religion, race, or ancestry, but by a core of shared ideals and values. Americans prize freedom, fairness, self-reliance, the open exchange of new ideas, and the contributions of new peoples.

★ They used to say the streets in America, most often referring to New York, were paved with gold. Well, they never really were paved with gold. But they are paved with opportunity.

★ Involvement in the world, and openness to new peoples, cultures, and ideas ensure a growing and dynamic society.

From the mayor's October 2001 Address to the United Nations:

★ There is no nation, and no city, in the history of the world that has seen more immigrants, in less time, than America. People continue to come here in large numbers to seek freedom, opportunity, decency, and civility.

39

The Spirit of New York

———————— ★ ————————

On explorer Henry Hudson's 1609 arrival:

★ I wonder if he had any idea that this would become the greatest city in the world.

★ The most visible symbol in New York is the spirit of a free people.

★ New York City is the capital of the world.

★ It is New York's diversity that makes us the greatest city in the world.

★ We've learned in our city if you expect more, you get it.

★ One of the keys to New York City's success throughout its history has been a willingness to embrace change.

★ New York City is a great functioning city. That's a wonderful thing.

★ We think of New York City as the financial capital of the world, and the publishing capital, but we don't always think of the city as the capital of compassion—and it is.

★ When things are bad, when times are tough, New Yorkers prove they are better and tougher.

★ New York City has always been a city in transition. And God willing, it always will be.

★ Fall is one of the best times of the year to be in New York City, because it is a time of anticipation, excitement, and celebration.

★ We know—all of us know—that this city is now the envy of the world. Let's keep it that way.

★ If you've got a problem with New York City being the capital of the world, take it up with the Pope.

★ New Yorkers always pull together when the going gets rough. Who can doubt our independent spirit . . . our self-reliance . . . our determination?

★ Problems are challenges to do better and prove just how talented, courageous, and exceptional the people of New York City really are.

★ We're not a separated city. We're not separated by race, religion, or ethnic background. We're not separated by borough. There is something that brings us together that is stronger, more powerful than all those differences. We are one, as proud New Yorkers.

★ When New York City is free to show its strengths to the rest of the country and the rest of the world, we do not disappoint. We excel.

★ The strength of New York City has been its ability to reinvent itself through the decades.

Airing the 1995 New York City tourism slogan on the Late Show *with David Letterman:*

★ We can kick your city's ass!

On New York City and immigration:

★ I believe that one of the secrets of New York's success—well, maybe not a secret, but something we don't always think enough about—is immigration. Over the past two centuries, people have come to this city from many different places, bringing different religions and different backgrounds. But they've all come with a common feeling and purpose: to make a better life for themselves and their families. That common purpose unites them as New Yorkers in a very special way.

★ You can't be a New Yorker—you can't be part of this city—and deny the contributions of immigrants.

★ When I see new people, I see new opportunities.

★ The fact is that America depends on New York and New York depends on immigration.

★ New York City's large immigrant population has always been a source of our strength. We have become the richest, most successful city in the world because of the energy and drive of immigrants who come here to create better lives for themselves and their children.

★ Immigration is the secret of our success. It's certainly the secret of New York's success. The spirit of our city is renewed over and over again by new people who come here wanting to make a better life for themselves and their families, and then they make life better for all of us.

★ For all the talk of redefinition and reformation, for all the talk about redefining government, do you know how New York City is redefined and reformed? Not by processes, not by abstractions, but by people, people from all over the world coming here to build a better life for themselves and their families.

★ In New York City, we have two of our country's most enduring symbols of hope, freedom, and opportunity—the Statue of Liberty and Ellis Island. These monuments are constant reminders of who we are and where we came from.

★ The doors to New York City are open to all people seeking renewal and redefinition, to all new people who come here to find a better life, and in so doing, renew us.

★ My grandparents made the same decision to come to New York. Actually, I sometimes think of my grandfather on the shores of Genoa with his little satchel in his hands, preparing to come to the New World. And now that Ellis Island has been given to New Jersey, I can't help but wonder if he was really saying to himself, "I'm going to New Jersey." Deep down, I know it was "New York."

★ There is no city more diverse than New York—and I believe that accounts for our strength and our success.

★ The reality of New York is much better than the perception of it.

★ New York's success is America's success and vice versa.

★ A city, and especially a city like New York, should be a place of optimism.

★ In attempting to appeal to reason and intellect rather than play to the fear and emotions of the American people, New York City has led the fight to uphold the sanctity of the core values upon which this country was built.

★ As a center of world trade, New York has always been open to different cultures—an openness that has produced a city like no other in the world. . . .

★ In New York City, if you're not sure of yourself, you really can't accomplish very much.

★ I think New Yorkers are essentially very, very nice people; they're not unlike the people in the rest of the country. And the only reason that we have a few more problems is we have a few more people.

★ We are the capital of the world, and the champions of the world, and it just doesn't get any better than that.

★ New Yorkers have always braved the hardships of life with a true flair.

On New York City employees:

★ As much as anything else, it's the dedication and professionalism of our city employees that make New York City the envy of every city in the world.

In praise of New York City's emergency personnel and city employees' response to a 2000 snowstorm:

★ In the wee hours of Saturday, December 30, snow started to fall on the city. New Yorkers love the way snow looks blanketing our lawns and city parks—particularly around Christmas—but when the snow starts to fall on our streets and avenues, people change their tune. And that's when New York City calls on its unsung heroes.

★ The public servants of our city have proven themselves to be a critical part of the life and spirit of New York. Their commitment to the city has been the foundation of our renaissance. Our historic crime reduction, reform of social services, and record job creation would not have been possible without them and their hard work.

On New York City culture:

★ It is in the music, drama, dance, paintings, sculpture, and architecture created, and in the writings of our philosophers, theologians, poets, novelists, and historians that we define ourselves for future generations—not only for future generations of New Yorkers, but of Americans and people around the world.

★ There is a spirit here that makes New York City the capital of the world. The most cursory summary includes Lincoln Center, Carnegie Hall, reliable and inexpensive public transportation (including charming ferries and a tram), many of the world's great museums, the Yankees, Mets, Rangers, and Knicks, the first-class universities, peerless theaters, lush parks, unbeatable restaurants, and the greatest, most generous citizens in the world.

★ There is an enormous purpose that cities serve. Without in any way minimizing the contributions other municipalities make to this country, it really is in cities that our culture developed. It is in cities in which the shows are performed that are performed fifty to one hundred years later. It is in cities that the operas are performed that people have performed for three hundred years. And it's largely in cities where a culture defines itself. In essence, a city is where people of talent, people of creativity in all different fields, can come together.

★ New York City's universities are some of the very, very best in the world. It always gets me annoyed when people think of Boston as kind of the college and university center of the United States. We have more universities (we've got a much better baseball team, too).

On Broadway theaters:

★ It's our single biggest tourist attraction . . . they're even a bigger tourist attraction than the Yankees and the Mets, which I don't admit very often, but they are.

When David Letterman thought of moving his Late Show *to California, in 1995, Giuliani urged otherwise.*

★ David Letterman has a great time with his show. What he has done in the middle of Broadway is terrific. I think his brand of humor really, really works in New York City. I think it's very peculiar to New York, and I think he'll remember that.

★ I think when he gets back here, in the clear air of New York, and he isn't affected by some of the pollution in Los Angeles that may have affected his judgment, he's going to feel very differently about it.

Reflecting on an evening out in August 2001 in his beloved New York City:

★ On the boat to Coney Island that evening in August, we curled around the Gowanus Bay and I spotted a familiar sight—a lady who for 115 years has reminded visitors and New Yorkers alike what this city means to the country and the world. The Statue of Liberty has long welcomed newcomers to the city of New York, and that beacon of freedom will always hold the promise of a better life.

Giuliani sharing the campaign introduced in November 2001 to encourage tourism in New York City:

★ The New York Miracle. Be a part of it.